Seeking Love in Every Season

Other Books

Gathering the Wayward Heart:
Lessons on Faith, Trust, and Surrendering Our Best-Laid Plans

Seeking Peace in Every Season:
12-Week Devotional, Journal, and Planner

We Get You! 30 Days, 30 Women, 30 Stories, One God

Seeking Love in Every Season

12-Week Devotional and Journal

Tracey Glenn

BEATITUDES PUBLISHING

SEEKING LOVE IN EVERY SEASON

Beatitudes Publishing

Paperback ISBN: 978-1-962581-26-4
Cover & Interior Design: Tracey Glenn

To every woman who seeks to feel loved in a world that doesn't know how to love.

To those who give love but don't receive it.

God sees you and loves you.

Contents

1 John 3:1 NLT

See how very much our Father loves us, for he calls us his children, and that is what we are! But the people who belong to this world don't recognize that we are God's children because they don't know him.

Forward

Congratulations! You are holding a book that will cheer you on, chant instead of rant, and challenge you to change the way you think of love and worth!

I met Tracey Glenn for the first time when she was in a room in a hotel next to me at the Christian Communicators Conference.

Her smile was soft and genuine. I could tell she was a woman who was passionate in a peace giving way about sharing God's love. She knew He loved her and what her worth was to Him.

As I watched her I noticed something different about her.

Love seeped out of her when she listened and it flowed from her when she spoke. I knew love was something she didn't take lightly when her husband sent flowers to her at the conference. Not just any kind of flowers, but one of the most beautiful rose bouquets I had ever seen. She knocked my fuzzy socks off when she left the flowers with me at the end of the conference. She could not fly on a plane with them so she shared the love with me. It worked. As a former school teacher turned speaker, I knew she had the ability to impact the younger generation as well as the older. Tracey has a youthful spark that can ignite a flame one person at a time.

Her writing is open, straightforward, and direct and this is what makes you turn each page desiring to read more. We shared the microphones again in 2023 and I hired her to create video work for me. She captured me with the camera the way God sees me.

She is kind of like the gal who is slow to speak but fast on the draw. She is full blood-Arizona bred reaching for the sky and living out a Holy high. She has the courage of a cowgirl and this bold boot wearing, heart baring, love sharing woman wants you and I to experience what she has discovered. Jesus. The joy of the Lord is her strength. This is the Tracey Glenn I know and love.

Now that we are talking about love, she wants to share with you about the love of God in this devotional. She knows what she is talking about and I am excited to see you dig in and grasp His love for you as He reveals this through the words in this book.

God fills in the gaps and gets us back in the saddle to ride life out better than we ever imagined.

You'll find the following as you read each day:

* Real turning points, pivots, and detours in life
* Funny Ahas!
* Love and lessons to help us live worthy of His call
* Meaningful stories meant to encourage

In a way, I envy the experience of the journey you're about to begin as you read and feast on the stories of Tracey's experiences and the lives of the people in the Bible. She makes it all so relatable.

It makes me look forward to reading her next book.

May you live life differently from this day forward as you ride into the sunset following the SON!

—Tammy Whitehurst, Motivational Speaker--TammyWhitehurst.com

God's love is like an ocean. You can see its beginning, but not its end.

—Rick Warren

Week One

Day One

1 Peter 4:8 NIV
Above all, love each other deeply,
because love covers a multitude of sins.

Study

We seek love from the world but are left feeling empty because love is a need that can't be fulfilled by anyone but God. As we study what the Bible says about God's agape love, we will examine how the world tries unsuccessfully to fill this need. The world can't give what it doesn't have.

The people in the Bible walked this earth just as you do, and they struggled with the same principalities of darkness that you fight against. We need to recognize and acknowledge this fact if we are going to make any progress on our journey of seeking love in our lives. It's the goal of evil to leave you feeling unwanted and unloved.

But love isn't a feeling—it's an act. It's something we must give to truly receive. Once we find healing, we find love. We heal when we no longer allow others to determine our worthiness of love. True love comes from God alone.

I am confident that when the Pharisees brought the woman caught in adultery to Jesus, she did not feel loved. As the eyes of contempt stared down at her, I can only imagine the thoughts racing through her head and the fear in her heart. The punishment for adultery was a death sentence by stoning.

As you journal today, think of a time when you felt ridiculed and unloved. How have you healed that memory? If you don't feel loved today, describe why you feel unloved.

Let's Pray

Father, I know I will never experience feeling loved apart from You. Please help me rely on You alone to fill the emptiness inside. Please help me stop seeking love from the world and turn to You. I want to be whole through You. In Jesus's name. Amen

Write It Out!

Reflect on what God is speaking to your heart today.

Date:________________________

Today I am feeling...

What one thing are you thankful for today?

Day Two

Matthew 5:44 NLT
But I say, love your enemies!
Pray for those who persecute you!

Study

When people wound you, you have a right to be angry. But don't allow others' actions to bind you with bitterness. It hurts you, not them.

Imagine the root of bitterness the woman at the well had cultivated in her life. There is no telling the trauma she experienced, and it reflected in her choices. She was rejected by others. As the other women went to the well in the cool morning, she went in the heat of the day. She was excluded from an activity that, in Biblical times, was the social highlight of a woman's day.[1] The enemy doesn't want us to forget our shortcomings. He uses the words and actions of others to bind us.

As a child, I was the only girl in my class not invited to a birthday party. I still remember standing in line for lunch, feeling unwanted and unloved, while the other girls chatted excitedly about the party. Those thoughts still make me uncomfortable. That day was a defining moment in my life, and I put myself back in that place, even now, when I look for approval from others instead of God.

Satan used the thoughtless action of one sinful human to bind me with feelings of inadequacy. But with God's grace, we can put those feelings behind us. When you rely on God to fill you with love, people's actions lose their sting.

As you journal today, what hurt do you need to surrender to God? Writing heals. I encourage you to reflect on your feelings and write without holding back.

Let's Pray

Father, I know I have difficulty letting go of others' hurtful actions. I realize negative feelings will never go away until I fully surrender them to You. Help me do this today as I lay these wounds at Your feet. Please heal me and make me whole, Lord. In Jesus's name. Amen.

Write It Out!

Reflect on what God is speaking to your heart today.

Date:__________________________

Today I am feeling...

What one thing are you thankful for today?

Day Three

Psalm 86:15 NLT
But you, O Lord, are a God of compassion and mercy, slow to get angry and filled with unfailing love and faithfulness.

Study

Imagine being completely excluded from society like the woman who bled for twelve years. In those days, due to Jewish law, she was not allowed to have contact with anyone. She was called "unclean." Can you imagine having that label forced upon you?

She lived in isolation. And after twelve years, she would have felt forgotten. But she had faith. She believed that Jesus could heal her, and she broke every rule to connect with Him. She not only wanted healing, but she also needed it. Her well-being depended on it.

Wanting and needing are two different things. I remember wanting a piece of candy in the store, but my mom told me I didn't need it. So, I did what I felt I had to do—I stole it. Thankfully, Mom discovered I took the candy and marched me back into the store. I remember trembling as I told the manager what I had done. But candy and love are two different things. No one needs a piece of candy, but we all need love. God made us that way.

When you are willing to do anything to feel loved, you fall into the trap of the enemy. Because when you need a person to give you your identity, you will never be who God says you are. Your identity is in Christ. Friend, you are a beloved, chosen, and treasured child of God (John 1:12, 1 Peter 2:9, Colossians 3:12).

As you journal today, write about who you are in Christ. God sees Jesus when He looks at you. Therefore, you are perfect in His sight.

Let's Pray

Father, I know I am wonderfully made. You do not make mistakes. Please help me find my identity in Your Word. Help me embrace Your love and know I will always be enough through You. I pray this in Jesus's name. Amen.

Write It Out!

Reflect on what God is speaking to your heart today.

Date:________________________

Today I am feeling...

What one thing are you thankful for today?

Day Four

Psalm 85:10 ESV
Steadfast love and faithfulness meet;
righteousness and peace kiss each other.

Study

When we accept Jesus as our Savior, we access His redeeming love. Jesus washes us clean, but we must lay down our sinful desires and clothe ourselves in His righteousness. It doesn't mean our memories are erased because there is still healing to be done, but it does mean we are a new creation (2 Corinthians 5:17).

If the woman at the well had refused her new identity, she would have been unable to tell others what Christ had done for her. The gift must be accepted to be received. That is the secret to love. You must accept that God has changed you.

When I was a young woman, I thought every boy I dated would be my husband. I was so desperate for love that I went looking for it. I craved love because I couldn't love myself. But I was looking in the wrong places. If I am honest with myself, I must admit that I was actually opposed to being loved because I wasn't attracted to the boys who showed me love—I was attracted to the ones who were impressive in the eyes of the world. Therefore, I received only shallow flattery and abuse from them. Like the woman at the well, I had to learn that no earthly man would ever be able to make me feel loved. Love comes from the seed God planted in every human's soul, and He is the only One who can water it and make it grow.

As you journal today, ponder this question. Do you feel loved or unloved today? Why?

Let's Pray

Father, I acknowledge that I will never feel loved by someone until I learn to love from within. You are the giver of life, and You alone make me feel loved. Please grow the seed of love You planted in my soul. Help me stop seeking and start receiving. I pray this in Jesus's name. Amen.

Write It Out!

Reflect on what God is speaking to your heart today.

Date:__________________________

Today I am feeling...

What one thing are you thankful for today?

Day Five

1 Corinthians 13:13 ESV
So now faith, hope, and love abide, these three;
but the greatest of these is love.

Study

The Holy Spirit gives all Christians three spiritual gifts: faith, hope, and love. These three attributes are a light to draw the unbeliever to the Lord. In Christ, we have faith and hope, and in love, we should want others to have what we have.

The woman who bled for twelve years had faith by hearing, not seeing. Her faith was so tremendous that she believed she only needed to touch the fringe of Jesus's garment to be healed. She wasn't seeking to be noticed—just healed. But things didn't go as planned because as soon as she touched His clothes, Jesus knew (Mark 5:30). At this point, every eye was on her.

When I was about twelve, I went on a trip with one of my sisters. We stopped to eat and sat in the smaller of two dining rooms. I needed to use the restroom, and as soon as I walked in the door, I knew something was wrong. I mistakenly walked into the men's restroom. Now, if the bathrooms had been down a long hall or tucked in a back corner, I could have walked out unnoticed. But the doors were right in the middle of the wall in the big dining room. I was mortified, and I knew there was no escaping unnoticed. I stepped out of the bathroom, and every eye was on me. Embarrassed, I just went and sat back at the table with my sister, who was oblivious. I made this moment one of many secret shames. Satan uses these moments to bind us.

As you journal today, think about a secret shame you are holding onto. Write it out and release it into the hands of Christ.

Let's Pray

Father, I am tired of allowing the enemy to use my shame against me. Please help me surrender the notion that I will be perfect because I know it's impossible. In Jesus's name, I pray. Amen.

Write It Out

Reflect on what God is speaking to your heart today.

Date:________________________

Today I am feeling...

What one thing are you thankful for today?

Day Six

Dig Deeper

Read the following passages: John 4:4–42; John 8:1–11; Mark 5:21–34.

Let's unpack the lives of the three women we discussed this week. Two of the women were products of their poor decisions, and the third had no control over her situation. Regardless, they were all looking for the same thing. They were searching for their identity in a cruel world. In society's eyes, they were all unclean.

We all have something the enemy uses against us. We all have a point of impact in our lives—something we are embarrassed about or ashamed of.

As he did with the Samaritan woman, satan uses the opinions and words of others to force us to gather water alone in the heat of the day. Her life experiences led to shame, which led to poor choices, which led to ridicule and isolation. Her inability to love herself caused her to avoid love from others. We do that also. When we feel we are unworthy and we don't embrace the love Christ gives, love feels uncomfortable. We seek and desire it, but we can't allow ourselves to receive it. It's a vicious cycle, and if satan can use it to bind us, he will.

When you identify the fear that holds you back, you are one step closer to identifying a stain on your soul. You are one step closer to embracing your identity in Christ.

As you journal today, think about a moment of impact in your life. What is the enemy using to silence you or keep you isolated?

Let's Pray

Father, You restored my soul and made me new when I came to know and accept You. However, the enemy works hard to never let me forget. Please help me use the moments that satan meant for evil for Your glory. Help me uncover his hidden schemes and step boldly into Your presence. I cannot rewrite the past, but I can surrender to Your will and trust You. You are the author of my future. In Jesus's name. Amen.

Write It Out!

Reflect on what God is speaking to your heart today.

Date:________________________

Today I am feeling...

What one thing are you thankful for today?

Day Seven

Today is a day to rest and reflect. This is a great day to complete the End of Week Goal Tracker and see your progress. Use the section below for sermon notes, rest in the Lord, and enjoy your family.

Write It Out!

Reflect on what God is speaking to your heart today.

Date:______________________

Sermon Notes:

Prayer Journal

What are you praying for? Write your prayers here. As your prayers are answered, jot down the day and how God answered. Was it what you prayed for or something better?

I am praying that God will…	Date	God answered by…

Who will you pray for this week?

Person/Organization:

Need:

Person/Organization:

Need:

The shape of true love isn't a diamond. It's a cross.

—*Alicia Bruxvoort*

Week Two

Day One

Romans 5:8 NLT
But God showed his great love for us
by sending Christ to die for us while we were still sinners.

Study

Before Jesus set her free, Mary Magdalene was possessed by seven demons (Luke 8:2). Christ made her a new creation. Mary Magdalene became someone Jesus trusted and loved. She was chosen as His.

If Jesus is your Savior, you are also trusted, loved, and chosen. Isn't that comforting to know? It means God is for you and will protect you. Because Jesus freed Mary, she was one of the women who stood close when He was crucified and the first to know of His resurrection. Jesus sent Mary to tell the others the good news (John 20:11–18). Mary was very important to Him, and so are you.

I grew up on a ranch where the nearest neighbors lived miles from our house. One of our neighbors set traps for predatory animals like coyotes. Because my dog Missy ran off a lot, one day, she was caught in this neighbor's trap. When he released her so she could go home, she jumped into the back of his pickup and right up on top of the cab. She was there to stay, and the only way he could get her off was to drive her home. I still remember him driving in as she clung to the cab of that pickup. It was quite a sight. It reminds me of our relationship with Jesus. Sin is a trap, and Jesus saves us and releases us. We must cling to Him so He can take us home. Isn't that a wonderful thought?

As you journal today, think about this question. What trap has Jesus released you from? Are you still holding onto the trap, or are you clinging to Jesus?

Let's Pray

Father, You are so faithful to forgive. Thank You for releasing me from the trap of sin. I ask You to reveal the things in me that displease You and help me break free from the chains the enemy places on me. In Jesus's name, I pray. Amen.

Write It Out!

Reflect on what God is speaking to your heart today.

Date:________________________

Today I am feeling...

What one thing are you thankful for today?

Day Two

Ephesians 2:4–5 NLT
But God is so rich in mercy, and he loved us so much,
that even though we were dead because of our sins,
he gave us life when he raised Christ from the dead.
(It is only by God's grace that you have been saved!)

Study

Love is a basic human need. According to psychologists, it is as basic a need as food and water.[2] Love is a human emotion designed by God to be demonstrated through selflessness, compassion, care, and affection toward others.

In pursuing love and acceptance, we allow fear to guide us. We see this in Judah's daughter-in-law Tamar's story found in Genesis 38. Tamar was twice widowed. She married Judah's son Er first, and after his death, she was given to Judah's son Onan, who also died. Judah's third son, Shelah, was too young to marry, so Judah sent Tamar back to her father to wait for Shelah. However, when Shelah was old enough, Judah didn't send for Tamar.

So, Tamar took matters into her own hands. After disguising herself as a prostitute, Tamar became pregnant by Judah. Reacting to emotion and taking matters into our own hands is never a display of trust in the Lord.

When we rush ahead of God and make a mess of things, we often deal with unlovely consequences. However, God is rich in mercy, and His will is always done regardless of how we mess things up.

As you journal today, answer this question: What is a situation you are trying to control in your life? How can you trust God?

Let's Pray

Father, I give every fear and situation into Your hands. Help me get out of the way and let You take control of my life. Your will and purpose are perfect. I trust You to lead me down the right path and work every situation for my good. In Jesus's name, I pray. Amen.

Write It Out!

Reflect on what God is speaking to your heart today.

Date:________________________

Today I am feeling...

What one thing are you thankful for today?

Day Three

Zephaniah 3:17 ESV
...he will rejoice over you with gladness; he will quiet you by his love; he will exult over you with loud singing.

Study

It's important we find our identity in Christ. It means life or death where eternity is concerned. In Genesis 16, we find Hagar's identity formed by her circumstances. She was an Egyptian slave to Abraham's wife, Sarah. Ten years passed after God gave Abraham the prophecy that he would be made a great nation. And after ten long years of Sarah not getting pregnant, she decided to take matters into her own hands. Sarah thought she could create her family through Hagar, and everything would be perfect. But it was far from perfect—it was disastrous.

Once the younger Hagar began to flaunt her pregnancy, Sarah became bitter toward Abraham and placed the blame on him. This account gives us several pearls of wisdom, one of which is not to covet what God gives others.

I went to school with a girl who I thought was gorgeous. I used to believe that if I looked like her, my life would be perfect. But her life wasn't perfect. She let the world determine her value. When boys told her she was ugly, she believed their words. Classic enemy strategy: attack us at our weakest point. I could see her perception of herself in her choices. I watched as her boyfriend chased her down to beat her up, and many years later, I saw an almost unrecognizable shell of an abused woman. She allowed a sinful human to determine her worth.

As you journal today, answer this question: What identity have you allowed others to place on you?

Let's Pray

Lord, I know I have allowed others to give me an identity that is contrary to who You say I am. Being Your child makes me valuable because I am the daughter of the King. Help me remember this today and be confident in who You say I am. In Jesus's name. Amen.

Write It Out!

Reflect on what God is speaking to your heart today.

Date:____________________________

Today I am feeling...

What one thing are you thankful for today?

Day Four

1 Corinthians 13:4–5 NIV
Love is patient, love is kind. It does not envy,
it does not boast, it is not proud.
It does not dishonor others, it is not self-seeking,
it is not easily angered, it keeps no record of wrongs.

Study

When we have no hope, we have no desire to live. And when we feel unloved, we have no desire to give love. Where love is absent, so is patience, kindness, forgiveness, and humility. Hagar is a perfect example of someone who felt unloved. Once she received a taste of what she perceived as love, she became boastful and proud. She flaunted her pregnancy before Sarah and stirred up wrath. Neither of the women in this account was loving toward the other.

We live in a world filled with people who feel unloved. The words and actions of others have created a worldwide epidemic of unloved, overreactive zombies. Maybe we really are living in a zombie apocalypse!

I know someone who fits this description. When she was a child, her parents lavished material possessions on her. However, as the sibling of a terminally ill child, she felt like she lacked attention and love. This made her bitter, and a root of bitterness grew deep. When her brother died, her bitterness grew toward her dad, and when her dad passed, she aimed it at her mom. The truth is, no one but God could fill the void in her life. No one will experience a love that fills every void without God because we all have a God-shaped hole in our souls.

As you journal today, think of someone who is lacking love. How can you show someone love today? Is there a void in your life that you need to ask God to fill?

Let's Pray

Father, I thank You for Your perfect love. I know there are so many hurting people because they lack love and are missing the key ingredient, which is You. Please fill me with Your perfect love and help me love others like You love me. I pray this in Jesus's name. Amen.

Write It Out!

Reflect on what God is speaking to your heart today.

Date:__________________________

Today I am feeling...

What one thing are you thankful for today?

Day Five

1 Corinthians 13:6–7 NIV
Love does not delight in evil but rejoices with the truth.
It always protects, always trusts, always hopes, always perseveres.

Study

When we allow the enemy to plant seeds of hate in our hearts, he grows roots of bitterness that weave their way into our souls. Hatred doesn't hurt the person who caused you pain—it hurts you. Yes, we have every right to be angry over our pain, but we can't allow it to further destroy us. Sarah heaped her bitterness toward Hagar on Abraham. We heap our bitterness on those closest to us, which only upsets our lives.

I worked with a lady once who allowed herself to be steeped in bitterness. She walked into a room, and it was as if a dark cloud descended over everyone. She used the guise of being someone who speaks her mind to say whatever she wanted, whenever she wanted, regardless of how hurtful it was. One question we should ask is, "Whose truth is being spoken?" Her statements were true based on her perception but not necessarily the truth. God wants us to be steeped in His truth and speak in kindness and love.

Bitterness and hatred don't serve anyone well because they are pits with slippery sides. You fall in when you allow yourself to go too close to the edge. Without the Holy Spirit's leading, finding a way out of the pit is impossible.

As you journal today, sit quietly and allow the Holy Spirit to speak to your heart. What is He nudging you to change today?

Let's Pray

Father, I am thankful for Your Spirit Who resides within me. Please help me follow His leading. Help me walk in humility as I seek to please You by showing loving-kindness to a broken world. In Jesus's name. Amen.

Write It Out!

Reflect on what God is speaking to your heart today.

Date:________________________

Today I am feeling...

What one thing are you thankful for today?

Day Six

Dig Deeper

Read more about the three women we discussed this past week in Luke 8:1–2, John 20:11–18, Genesis 38, Genesis 16, Genesis 21.

Each woman's circumstance drove her perspective. When we can't let go of the hurt of our past, we live in the pit of despair.

In my book, *Gathering the Wayward Heart,* I wrote about suddenly losing my mom. It wasn't until she was gone that I realized how much I relied on her. Losing her left a void no one else could fill.

I could have used that loss to become bitter. But who would that have served? It wouldn't have served me or anyone around me. So, I chose to be thankful. I am thankful I had a great mom who taught me so many things and gave me so many wonderful memories. I am thankful I was with her for the last nine days of her life, and I had her for forty-two years.

Friend, I don't know what you have been through in your life. I don't know the pain others have caused you, but I know you have a God who loves you. If you are struggling with feeling unloved, please know I was there also. I had a great mom, but as others wounded me, I let the world define me.

As I drew closer to the Lord, God reminded me that He gave His life for the people who brutally beat and murdered Him. While most of those people didn't appreciate it, He knew we would. He knew we would be healed through His sacrifice.

As you journal today, write about your pain. Pour your heart out to God. If you're angry, say you're angry, and if you're wounded, acknowledge the pain. We serve a mighty God.

Let's Pray

Father, you know everything about me. You know my pain, and I acknowledge the fact that I am broken. Please heal my heart and help my wounds become scars. I pray this in Jesus's name. Amen.

Write It Out!

Reflect on what God is speaking to your heart today.

Date:__________________________

Today I am feeling...

What one thing are you thankful for today?

Day Seven

Today is a day to rest and reflect. This is a great day to complete the End of Week Goal Tracker and see your progress. Use the section below for sermon notes, rest in the Lord, and enjoy your family.

Write It Out!

Reflect on what God is speaking to your heart today.

Date:________________________

Sermon Notes:

Prayer Journal

What are you praying for? Write your prayers here. As your prayers are answered, jot down the day and how God answered. Was it what you prayed for or something better?

I am praying that God will…	Date	God answered by…

Who will you pray for this week?

Person/Organization:

Need:

Person/Organization:

Need:

Though our feelings come and go,
God's love for us does not.

—C.S. Lewis

Week Three

Day One

Mark 12:30 NKJV
And you shall love the LORD your God
with all your heart, with all your soul,
with all your mind, and with all your strength.
This is the first commandment.

Study

Like Ruth and Orpah found in the book of Ruth, we are never in control of our circumstances. We only control how we perceive and react to them. Initially, Ruth and Orpah chose to follow Naomi even though she encouraged them to return to their people. However, when she tried to convince them to leave her, only Ruth chose to stay. Ruth made a profound statement when she said, "Your people shall be my people, and your God, my God." (Ruth 1:16 NKJV). Ruth was choosing God in the face of uncertainty. Just like us, Ruth didn't know the end of her story. She had to have love and faith as she followed her mother-in-law to a land, people, and God she didn't know.

When we stand at a crossroads in life, we must have faith. However, we can't just stand looking and scratching our heads, wondering which way to go. The only way we can make an accurate decision is with prayer. Which road does God want us to take? We may not get an immediate answer to the question, but one thing's for certain: we must never give up.

Because God loves us, He provided a way for us to be saved. So many choose the other path, but you chose the right path.

As you journal today, acknowledge how God is caring for you. What amazing things has He done in your life?

Let's Pray

Father, Your love is beyond measure. The care You provide is perfect. Please help me rest in the peace of knowing You are in control of every situation. I trust You will work everything to my benefit. In Jesus's name, I pray. Amen.

Write It Out!

Reflect on what God is speaking to your heart today.

Date:__________________________

Today I am feeling...

What one thing are you thankful for today?

Day Two

Romans 12:9 NKJV
Let love be without hypocrisy.
Abhor what is evil. Cling to what is good.

Study

This life consists of two choices, and there are only two sides—right from wrong and good versus evil. There is no in-between.

We must choose what is right or wrong. In 1 Samuel 25, we find a woman who chose right. Her name was Abigail. Now, Abigail was married to a very wealthy but wicked man named Nabal. When David fled from King Saul, he sent his men to Nabal with a simple request for food and shelter. Through his men, David reminded Nabal of the kindness shown him and asked for that kindness to be reciprocated. In 1 Samuel 25:10–11, we read Nabal's hostile response.

Because of Nabal's response, David set out to kill every male associated with Nabal's house. Putting her life on the line, Abigail intervened. Her righteousness was displayed in her selfless intercession on behalf of a wretched sinner. Through her actions, Abigail not only saved Nabal and his men, but she also stopped David from sinning in his anger. Her action reflects the love Christ showed us when He willingly died to pay for the consequences of our sins.[3]

There is only one choice of who we will serve. Will it be God or satan? I am so on God's side that I refuse to capitalize the enemy's name. God's side requires loyalty and difficult decisions, but we rest in His love and protection.

As you journal today, think about those who are hard to love. It is likely that some of them have hurt you. If you can, write out what they did and give it to God. Writing is healing.

Let's Pray

Father, please help me heal from the pain difficult people have caused me. Help me cast my cares upon You as I journal my feelings. I pray this in Jesus's name. Amen.

Write It Out!

Reflect on what God is speaking to your heart today.

Date:__________________________

Today I am feeling...

What one thing are you thankful for today?

Day Three

Romans 12:10 NLT
Love each other with genuine affection,
and take delight in honoring each other.

Study

An overwhelming desire for attention, recognition, power, money, or anything we deem valuable is a lure from the enemy that leads us to a pit of brokenness. I have always struggled with a need for attention, and satan caught me in that slippery pit more than I want to admit.

The attention trap is the fate of Gomer in the book of Hosea. When God instructed Hosea to marry the promiscuous woman, Gomer, Hosea obeyed. He was aware of her tendencies when he chose to do what God asked of him.[4]

The movie *Amazing Love: The Story of Hosea* gives a great perspective on the book of Hosea. After Gomer left Hosea to live with another man, she got comfortable in her position and dared to refuse a request from him. As a result, he ordered his guards take her away and auction her off. We see a broken and bruised Gomer stripped of her dignity. At the auction, no one but Hosea saw her as valuable. He bought her back.

This is what God did for us. We chase after idols that we think will make us happy, and when we are battered and broken, God awaits us with open arms. Jesus bought us with His precious blood. Getting mad at God for the trials that come from our poor decisions would be like Gomer getting mad at Hosea because she left him. I don't know about you, but I have made some poor choices in my lifetime. Since we can't change the past, we must repent and change the future.

As you journal today, answer this question: How will you begin to change your future?

Let's Pray

Lord, I am so thankful for the love You have shown me. Thank You for forgiveness and Your redeeming grace. Help me rely solely on You and not chase after worthless idols. In Jesus's name, I pray. Amen.

Write It Out!

Reflect on what God is speaking to your heart today.

Date:__________________________

Today I am feeling...

What one thing are you thankful for today?

Day Four

1 Corinthians 10:13 ESV
No temptation has overtaken you that is not common to man. God is faithful, and he will not let you be tempted beyond your ability, but with the temptation he will also provide the way of escape, that you may be able to endure it.

Study

Our faith determines our choices. When we lack faith, we make decisions based on what our emotions tell us to do. Of the four women we studied this week, two acted on faith, and two on feelings. Orpah acted on fear, and Gomer on want.

We can all relate, right? It's the thought that if I only had that new job, new house, new boyfriend, or many other worldly things, I would be happy. It is a never-ending desire to be filled. The problem is, if left unchecked, there will always be something or someone better. God knows we will be tempted, and He always helps when we call on Him.

I remember standing in the grocery store one day when one of the employees walked behind me. As he walked behind me, he turned and started walking backward, checking me out. When I looked at him, he smiled and seemed happy at what he perceived as my interest. I'm not going to lie—since he was rather attractive and considerably younger than me, I was flattered.

As the weeks passed, I found myself seeing him at the store more often. Before I knew it, I was looking forward to bumping into him. I was daring to get closer and closer to the pit satan was preparing for me. Left unchecked, this would have been a scenario that led to disaster. We will never be happy chasing after sin.

As you journal today, answer this question: What does satan use to attempt to trap you?

Let's Pray

Lord, please help me seek Your will on every occasion. Help me yield to Your guidance today and every day. I know the world will try to tempt me, but I trust in Your deliverance. In Jesus's name. Amen.

Write It Out

Reflect on what God is speaking to your heart today.

Date:__________________________

Today I am feeling...

What one thing are you thankful for today?

Day Five

1 John 4:17 NLT
And as we live in God, our love grows more perfect.
So we will not be afraid on the day of judgment,
but we can face him with confidence
because we live like Jesus here in this world.

Study

God never forces us to comply. We must willingly follow. I can only imagine the doubt the enemy placed in Ruth and Abigail's thoughts. He will do anything to derail God's plan. I hear him now. "Are you sure you want to do that, Ruth? What if you travel all that way and things fall apart?" Abigail likely heard, "What if David decides to kill you? Are you sure you want to take that risk?"

I was facing the opposite with the grocery store guy. Satan was trying to use my ego, not doubt, to bring me down. Every time I ran into him, he approached me with flattery. A cat following a string comes to mind. The cat doesn't see anything but that string.

So how did I escape? I literally escaped with prayer. I remember pulling into the parking lot and saying, "God, You know my weaknesses. Please help me." It's funny because as soon as I stepped out of my car, there he was. I don't remember the words that came out of his mouth, but they repulsed me. Suddenly, it was as if my eyes were opened, and I stood there thinking, *what attracted you to this guy?* and *What was I doing?* Satan is a master at blinding us. We need God's perspective to see the truth.

As you journal today, think of something in your life that needs God's perspective. Write about it and release it to Him.

Let's Pray

Father, You know me better than I know myself. And You know the schemes the enemy uses to sideline me. Please open my eyes to his tactics. Please help me see everything he uses to keep me from Your will. I pray this in Jesus's name. Amen.

Write It Out!

Reflect on what God is speaking to your heart today.

Date:________________________

Today I am feeling...

What one thing are you thankful for today?

Day Six

Dig Deeper

Read Ruth 2:1–12.

Do you believe in divine intervention? How amazing is it that God sent Ruth to the field Boaz owned and caused him to notice and help her? This is how God works in the lives of those who know and love Him. However, Ruth had to be willing to humble herself.

Read 1 Samuel 25.

The account of Abigail is also a lesson on humility and action. God used her to stop David from acting out of anger and doing something he would later regret.

On the opposite end of the spectrum, we find Gomer. She was prideful and refused to be humble. It's interesting to note that Ruth and Abigail went from a bad situation that God made good, while Gomer took God's good situation and made it bad.

Throwing God's goodness away is human nature. A Hallmark movie called *The Magic of Ordinary Days* is the story of a young single woman named Olivia, Livy for short, who become pregnant in the 1940s. Her father found a young man named Ray, who was willing to marry her. So, she traveled a long distance by train, talked with Ray for a few minutes, and then they married. It is an inspiring movie that shows God's mercy even when we are living through the consequences of poor choices. However, Livy had difficulty seeing God's goodness in what she perceived as negative.

As you journal today, write about a situation that didn't go as you planned. How did it turn out? How can you view life differently today?

Let's Pray

Lord, You know what is best for me, and unlike a human father, Your will is always perfect. You never make a mistake. Please help me remember Your goodness in all situations. Help me see Your hand, which works everything to my good. Help me appreciate what I have by not desiring something I think is better. In Jesus's name I pray. Amen.

Write It Out!

Reflect on what God is speaking to your heart today.

Date:____________________________

Today I am feeling...

What one thing are you thankful for today?

Day Seven

Today is a day to rest and reflect. This is a great day to complete the End of Week Goal Tracker and see your progress. Use the section below for sermon notes, rest in the Lord, and enjoy your family.

Write It Out!

Reflect on what God is speaking to your heart today.

Date:________________________

Sermon Notes:

Prayer Journal

What are you praying for? Write your prayers here. As your prayers are answered, jot down the day and how God answered. Was it what you prayed for or something better?

I am praying that God will…	Date	God answered by…

Who will you pray for this week?

Person/Organization:

Need:

Person/Organization:

Need:

No matter what storm you face, you need to know that God loves you. He has not abandoned you.

—Franklin Graham

Week Four

Day One

Hebrews 12:6 NLT
For the Lord disciplines those he loves,
and he punishes each one he accepts as his child.

Study

Regardless of how we feel about consequences, good or bad, they are a part of life. When we are not corrected, we slip into small, seemingly insignificant sin habits. It can start as a tiny misstep and grow into actions that ruin a life. Sin penetrates and invades like a virus.

This is the state of Jericho in the book of Joshua. The Canaanites burned their children as a sacrifice to their false god Molech. They practiced idolatry, sodomy, and numerous other despicable things.[5]

Rahab lived amid all this evil. She was a street-smart prostitute with great powers of perception. Everyone heard of God's army, and they lived in fear of them for forty years.[6] But Rahab had faith. Not a faith that comes from knowing God because she was not brought up in a believing family. Her family was as lost as the rest of the Canaanites. Rahab had singular faith. She was chosen and called by God's grace.[7]

We can't let our circumstances dictate our choices. In *Dolly Parton's Christmas of Many Colors: Circle of Love*, her family praised God when they faced a dire situation. The mom and kids were trapped in their house after a blizzard covered it in snow. They could not get out, and they were slowly freezing to death. Dolly's mom did the only thing she knew to do; she gathered all the children in a circle and praised God through song. Through what Dolly noted as a miracle from God, the family was saved.

As you journal today, write about a miracle you experienced or heard about.

Let's Pray

Father, thank You for the protection You place over me daily. I know You are the God of miracles, and I trust You in every circumstance. In Jesus's name, I pray. Amen.

Write It Out!

Reflect on what God is speaking to your heart today.

Date:____________________________

Today I am feeling...

What one thing are you thankful for today?

Day Two

Psalm 147:3 NIV
He heals the brokenhearted
and binds up their wounds.

Study

Why do we want to be loved so badly that we will do anything to get it? We tend to abandon reality when we seek love. The feelings associated with "falling in love" are fleeting. We falsely believe those "butterflies" will last forever. The reality is they don't.

I often wonder what Leah thought when her father deceitfully used her in place of her sister, Rachel. Imagine the heartbreak she must have felt when Jacob realized he was tricked into marrying the wrong girl. Instead of getting his beautiful Rachel, he woke up next to a less desirable Leah. Think of the words spoken and the damage they likely caused her. His outrage and words probably made her feel unworthy and unloved. She likely felt like trash next to her beautiful sister, Rachel. *Used* and *discarded* come to mind—first by her father, then by Jacob.

In the movie, *The Magic of Ordinary Days,* which I mentioned last week, Livy's choices forced her to marry a stranger. She entered the marriage believing that once the real father found out about the baby, he would rush to rescue her. Even though the man she married was extremely kind to her, her pride caused her to miss God's goodness. Like Leah, she allowed her ideals to blind her to God's kindness. It's our perspective, not circumstances, that make us content.

As you journal today, expand on the blessing that came from a disappointment. Use a new perspective to find one good thing that happened from a disappointment.

Let's Pray

Lord, I know the enemy keeps me from seeing Your goodness. Please help me remember You watch over me. Help me see every circumstance through the lens of Your kindness. In Jesus's name. Amen.

Write It Out!

Reflect on what God is speaking to your heart today.

Date:__________________________

Today I am feeling...

What one thing are you thankful for today?

Day Three

1 John 4:8 ESV
Anyone who does not love
does not know God,
because God is love.

Study

God is love, and without Him, we can never experience true love. Love through God is patient, kind, humble, trusting, and always hopeful (1 Cor. 13:4–7). Therefore, when we look for love in a nonbeliever, we never find God's love. The wicked leave us feeling used and broken.

In 2 Samuel 13:1–22, we read about David's daughter Tamar. She was Absalom's sister, and the Bible says she was a beautiful virgin. Absalom and Tamar had a half-brother named Amnon, who was infatuated with Tamar and lusted after her obsessively. When he confided his desire to a friend, his friend helped him trap her. Amnon isolated Tamar and raped her. Afterward, the Bible says, "he hated her even more than he had loved her" (2 Samuel 13:15 NIV).

I experienced this when a boy pursue me. He told me what I wanted to hear and set a trap for me. In trust, I placed myself in a compromising position, and he date-raped me. Like Tamar, I could not escape. Once he had what he wanted, he threw me away like a piece of trash. Unlike Tamar, who publicly displayed her shame, I kept mine hidden. I let it become a weapon for the enemy to use against me. But, years later, I reflect on this event and still see God's grace. I see His love, and I am thankful.

As you journal today, write about a life-altering decision you made. How can you see God's grace regardless of the consequences?

Let's Pray

Lord, I am thankful You give us free will. I know I haven't always chosen wisely, but I know when I seek Your will in Your Word, my choices align with Your plan for my life. Help me remember to seek Your guidance in every circumstance. In Jesus's name. Amen.

Write It Out!

Reflect on what God is speaking to your heart today.

Date:_______________________

Today I am feeling...

What one thing are you thankful for today?

Day Four

Colossians 3:14 ESV
And above all these put on love,
which binds everything together in perfect harmony.

Study

When we look at our circumstances, we need to acknowledge God's grace and our choices. It's never too late to see things in a different light and change our course. Biblical love isn't just the love we show a spouse or loved one—it is the love we show humanity. It is how we show patience, kindness, and humility, even to those who are difficult to love. It reflects the love God gives us. We are supposed to be a light to the world, and we shine through love.

Humans are broken creatures with sinful natures, but God still shows us grace and mercy. Tamar's rape was inexcusable, as was the treatment Leah received from Jacob and her father, but they still had reasons to be thankful. Rahab and her family lost their whole society, but by God's grace, they were saved from destruction. We don't have control over every aspect of our lives, but we determine our reactions.

In the movie *The Magic of Ordinary Days*, Livy's sister, Abby, came up with ideas to free Livy from her situation. However, Abby's motives were self-serving. Her husband was deployed to fight in the war, and she was lonely. To ease her loneliness, she tried to talk Livy into spreading the rumor that Ray was an abusive drunk and was, therefore, leaving him. If Livy's morals had been as lacking as Abby's, she would have destroyed Ray's reputation without blinking an eye.

As you journal today, ask God to help you see your circumstances in a new light. What good has come from trials in your life?

Let's Pray

Lord, I know You show us grace in every circumstance. Please forgive me for doubting. Help me speak encouraging words that lift others up and help them through their trial. In Jesus's name. Amen.

Write It Out

Reflect on what God is speaking to your heart today.

Date:____________________________

Today I am feeling...

What one thing are you thankful for today?

Day Five

Ephesians 2:10 NLT
For we are God's masterpiece. He has created us anew in Christ Jesus, so we can do the good things he planned for us long ago.

Study

Our attitude toward our circumstances plays a big role in our quality of life. When we are dealt a disappointing hand, we must avoid the temptation to fold. We can't walk away every time things get tough.

I imagine Leah wanted to scream "foul" when Jacob reacted adversely to their marriage and then again when, one short week later, Jacob married Rachel. Leah had always been considered subpar to Rachel, and now it was on display in a big way. She had to share the rest of her life and her husband with her sister. In one short week, she lost her new identity, position, and dignity. But God didn't forget Leah. God blessed Leah with many children, and yet she still wasn't happy. No matter how many children she had, she never felt like she was enough. It wasn't just her circumstances—it was her perspective.

Livy didn't feel like Ray was the man of her dreams in *The Magic of Ordinary Days.* Day after day, she went through life guarded while, in vain, Ray did everything he could to win her love. For the first time in six months, Ray kissed his wife. When her response was stiff, he asked, "Is there anything you like about me, Livy?" When we constantly look for something better, we miss God's blessings.

As you journal today, write about how different life would be without a certain blessing. What blessing have you missed in pursuit of something better?

Let's Pray

Father, help me see my blessings. I thank You for each of them, and I want to appreciate what You give to me. Help me see You in every ordinary day. In Jesus's name. Amen.

Write It Out!

Reflect on what God is speaking to your heart today.

Date:________________________

Today I am feeling...

What one thing are you thankful for today?

Day Six

Dig Deeper

Read Ruth 3:2–5, 1 Samuel 25:23–24, and Hosea 2:7–8.

When we read about Ruth and Abigail, we see a reflection of who we need to be in Christ. Ruth and Abigail humbled themselves—not to be doormats, but to be intercessors. Gomer, on the other hand, was full of pride and lust for what the world would give her. James 4:4 NLT says, "If you want to be a friend of the world, you make yourself an enemy of God." The enemy uses our pride to lead us away from God and down a path of destruction.

In *The Magic of Ordinary Days*, Livy reached the edge of the pit she was about to fall into. After Ray asked her about her feelings for him, she asked, "Would it be better if I leave?" At this point, she was still placing hope in the father of her child. However, Livy's eyes were opened when she finally read the letter. It wasn't a love letter. Spoiler alert: the other guy didn't want her or the baby.

The Bible is God's love letter to us. God truly loves you. And like the Lord showed mercy to Gomer, He shows us mercy. He is a loving Father who blesses us with His amazing grace.

But we can't make the right decisions if we don't read the letter first. When you look at life through the lens of Christ by reading God's Word, you realize you are surrounded by love.

As you journal today, examine your relationship with the Lord. How often do you read your Bible or sit and truly enjoy the presence of God? Ask God to help you discover ways to seek Him.

Let's Pray

Father, I desire to draw closer to You daily. Help me see Your love as I study Your Word. Please help me see myself and others through Your lens. Help me see the way You see and love the way You love. I pray Your love will shine through me. I pray this in Jesus's name. Amen.

Write It Out!

Reflect on what God is speaking to your heart today.

Date:________________________

Today I am feeling...

What one thing are you thankful for today?

Day Seven

Today is a day to rest and reflect. This is a great day to complete the End of Week Goal Tracker and see your progress. Use the section below for sermon notes, rest in the Lord, and enjoy your family.

Write It Out!

Reflect on what God is speaking to your heart today.

Date:________________________

Sermon Notes:

Prayer Journal

What are you praying for? Write your prayers here. As your prayers are answered, jot down the day and how God answered. Was it what you prayed for or something better?

I am praying that God will...	Date	God answered by...

Who will you pray for this week?

Person/Organization:

Need:

Person/Organization:

Need:

God loves us too much to indulge our every whim.

—Max Lucado

Week Five

Day One

1 John 4:7 ESV
Beloved, let us love one another, for love is from God, and whoever loves has been born of God and knows God.

Study

Let's look at the great love between Sarah and Abraham, first known as Sarai and Abram. The Lord protected and blessed them, and by the time they returned to Israel, they were very wealthy. They were rich in every way except for children. Sarah was barren, and nothing she did could change that fact. So, Sarah decided to take matters into her own hands. I guess she thought God needed a little help. But Sarah's "solution" caused turmoil in their home. Sarah began to doubt Abraham's love. How often do we think God needs some direction and help? We decide we know best, and in our efforts, we make a mess of things.

In the movie *Coat of Many Colors,* Dolly's mom made her a coat from a blanket she made for their baby, who died shortly after birth. Sewing the coat helped her mother deal with her grief. Dolly loved the coat and wanted to make a grand entrance at school. She anticipated all the kids would be jealous. However, the kids at school didn't see the beauty in her coat. They laughed at her. The public shame changed Dolly's perspective. She began to see the coat as ugly. Then, like Sarah, those feelings of shame turned to anger toward her mother. The lies racing through her thoughts made her lash out at the one who truly loved her. Sometimes, we lash out at the only One who truly loves us, God.

As you journal today, write about a time you were disappointed or embarrassed and how you reacted to that situation.

Let's Pray

Father, it can be easy to lash out at those we love most—to react to our feelings and forget their love for us. Help me react in love. Please help me remember the enemy tries to make me react this way. Help me avoid his trap. In Jesus's name. Amen.

Write It Out!

Reflect on what God is speaking to your heart today.

Date:___________________________

Today I am feeling...

What one thing are you thankful for today?

Day Two

1 John 4:19 NIV
We love because he first loved us.

Study

The Five Love Languages, a well-known book by Gary Chapman, explores the idea that we all have different love languages. When someone doesn't speak our love language, we don't feel loved by them. They also don't feel loved by us. It's like when we speak only English and try to communicate with someone who doesn't speak English. There is no understanding.[8] Let's face it—if we can't communicate love to those around us, they can't receive it or give it back. Remember, love is an action, not an emotion. We can't experience love if we don't give love.

Sarah may have been loved by Abraham, but she likely didn't feel loved. Because of want, she was overlooking the blessings in her life. Those feelings are hard to overcome, and disappointment can easily turn to bitterness, especially when communication isn't going well.

When you buy into the enemy's lie that love is an emotion, he does everything in his power to make the actions and words of others cause you to feel unloved.

I will never forget fighting my way out from underneath a group of boys whose intent was to disrobe me. The fact that my boyfriend sat only five feet away playing a video game and couldn't care less didn't exude love. I made it out intact, and when I said something to him about his lack of concern, his response was, "You're not worth saving." Can you imagine how unloved I would have been if I had chosen him?

As you journal today, identify ways you give and receive love. Do you feel loved?

Let's Pray

Father, I am thankful for Your loving-kindness. I can love because You first loved me. Thank You for the times You have intervened in my life and saved me from my misled desires. In Jesus's name. Amen.

Write It Out

Reflect on what God is speaking to your heart today.

Date:________________________

Today I am feeling...

What one thing are you thankful for today?

Day Three

1 Corinthians 16:14 NKJV
Let all that you do be done with love.

Study

I can imagine that Sarah was a bit hard to love in her distress over her inability to conceive. She wanted things fixed, and she thought she had the power to do this.

I've always noticed that when I want something I can't obtain easily, it becomes the center of my focus. It is all I think about. That is how Sarah became. She was consumed with her desire for a child and the fact she was barren. So, to fix it, she sent Abraham to her servant Hagar. She thought anything would be better than what she currently had.

I remember thinking this way when I was a kid. I was so certain that if I could have my own horse, everything would be perfect.

I imagine Sarah thought similarly. She pictured herself stepping into the role of mother and holding her baby. Everything would be perfect when she had a child. The problem was it wasn't her baby.

Like my horse, who was a mean demon that bit and kicked me, Hagar was spiteful to Sarah. She refused to let Sarah forget that she was subpar because she couldn't conceive. Nothing could change the fact that it was Hagar's child, not Sarah's.

When we try to fix things for God, nothing works as planned.

As you journal today, write about unmet expectations. What is something you thought would make your life perfect, but it didn't?

Let's Pray

Father, You know what is best for me. There are things that I believed would make me happy, but now I know they were curses, not blessings. Please help me remember to wait for Your timing. Help me trust You in every way. In Jesus's name, I pray. Amen.

Write It Out!

Reflect on what God is speaking to your heart today.

Date:___________________________

Today I am feeling...

What one thing are you thankful for today?

Day Four

Mark 12:30 NLT
And you must love the Lord your God with all your heart, all your soul, all your mind, and all your strength.

Study

I like to follow the advice, "Be careful what you wish for, because you may get it."

This is where we find Sarah in Genesis 16. She got what she wanted, but she forgot to add Hagar into the equation. A now pregnant Hagar walked around with a smug look on her face. She actually looked down on Sarah. After all, in Hagar's mind, she was the better woman. She was fertile, and in those days, that meant everything in the eyes of the world. Sarah had no control over her situation.

A book written by Shannon Popkin titled *Control Girl* speaks about women's desire to take charge of life circumstances. Shannon points out a very interesting correlation between Eve and Sarah in the Bible. Both women convinced their husbands that their way, not God's, was the best way.[9] Pride always leads us in the wrong direction.

Have you ever pridefully convinced yourself, or someone else, that you knew what was best only to have things not work out? I know I have. There were several occasions in the early days of our business when I thought I had a perfect solution for a problem. However, as time passed, I often found my "solution" became a problem of its own.

As you journal today, write about how being humble makes you feel. Is there a relationship in your life that needs some humility?

Let's Pray

Lord, I know when I am hurt, I tend to put a wall up for protection. It can be difficult to tear those walls down, especially when I fear the consequences. Pride makes me believe I can protect myself, which separates me from love. Help me trust in Your protection, Father. I thank You, Jesus, and pray in Your name. Amen.

Write It Out!

Reflect on what God is speaking to your heart today.

Date:________________________

Today I am feeling...

What one thing are you thankful for today?

Day Five

1 John 4:16 NLT
We know how much God loves us,
and we have put our trust in his love.

Study

The wait was long for Sarah, but the Lord had a plan. It didn't matter how hard Sarah tried to alter the plan—it wouldn't change until God was ready to change it.

As sinful humans, we tend to believe that God will bless everyone equally. That's why prosperity preachers get rich from exploiting the promises of God. We want to forget that He has a different plan for each of us. Just as it is not God's will to heal everyone (2 Corinthians 12:7–9), certain things may not be His will for you.

My middle child has special needs and health issues resulting from those needs. I went through a brief period when I fell into listening to the prosperity gospel and prayed relentlessly for God to heal her. However, no matter how hard I prayed, He would not heal her because it was not His plan. I remember sitting in church and listening to a sermon on Paul. Paul had an affliction that God wouldn't remove. The Lord told Paul, "My grace is sufficient for you, for my power is made perfect in weakness" (2 Cor. 12:9 NIV). I felt God saying, "Be thankful for the blessings I have given you."

Gratitude is directly linked to optimism.[10] When we are thankful, we live a longer and happier life. When I forget to thank God for my blessings, I see fault in everything around me.

As you journal today, express gratitude for your blessings. Is there a situation in your life that needs a gratitude adjustment?

Let's Pray

Father, I know I sometimes forget to be thankful for the blessings You place on my life. Please help me realize when I need a gratitude adjustment. Show me ways to lift others up and help them see the blessings You've placed in their lives. In Jesus's name. Amen.

Write It Out

Reflect on what God is speaking to your heart today.

Date:________________________

Today I am feeling...

What one thing are you thankful for today?

Day Six

Dig Deeper

Read Genesis 17:15–22 and Genesis 18:1–15.

Sarah and Abraham waited ten years before Sarah sent Abraham to Hagar. After Hagar had her baby, they waited another thirteen years before God reaffirmed His promise.[11] However, even when the baby came, Sarah's life wasn't perfect—she still had to deal with Hagar and her son.

When Abraham made Hagar and her son leave, I can imagine the smile on Sarah's face as she watched them go. She had rid herself of them, but the thoughts and feelings left in their wake likely stuck with her. Without forgiveness, situations like this can plague us for years.

It is okay to be angry, but we can't let it bind us (Eph. 4:26). We need to heal. When we look to God, we are filled with perfect love—not a love based on emotions, but a filling love expressed by action. Showing love to others through kindness, compassion, and forgiveness fills us with God's love, even if it's loving at a distance.

There is someone in my life who I love at a distance. This person attempted to divide my family. She tried to turn my daughter and husband against me. The ripples from our fallout were wide, and for years, I refused to forgive her. The road to forgiveness was difficult, but I had to let go of the hurt that turned to bitterness. I had to trust that God would help me heal. I couldn't control what she did, but I could control myself. God healed my heart.

As you journal today, write about what forgiveness means to you. If you are having a difficult time forgiving, write about it. Ask God for His help and what He wants you to do.

Let's Pray

Father, I know that unforgiveness is a bottomless pit of despair. There is victory in the act of forgiveness because the enemy can no longer use those feelings to bind me in bitterness. Help me claim the peace and love that comes from forgiving. In Jesus's name. Amen.

Write It Out!

Reflect on what God is speaking to your heart today.

Date:__________________________

Today I am feeling...

What one thing are you thankful for today?

Day Seven

Today is a day to rest and reflect. This is a great day to complete the End of Week Goal Tracker and see your progress. Use the section below for sermon notes, rest in the Lord, and enjoy your family.

Write It Out!

Reflect on what God is speaking to your heart today.

Date:____________________

Sermon Notes:

Prayer Journal

What are you praying for? Write your prayers here. As your prayers are answered, jot down the day and how God answered. Was it what you prayed for or something better?

I am praying that God will…	Date	God answered by…

Who will you pray for this week?

Person/Organization:

Need:

Person/Organization:

Need:

*"God and love are synonymous.
Love is not an attribute of God,
it is God; whatever God is, love is."*

—*Oswald Chambers*

Week Six

Day One

Jeremiah 31:3 NIV
I have loved you with an everlasting love;
I have drawn you with unfailing kindness.

Study

God loves you with everlasting love, and He draws you close to Him with unfailing kindness. God is as much alive and active today as He was in the accounts of the Bible thousands of years ago.

In Genesis 24, we are given a glimpse of the power of prayer. Abraham sent his servant to Nahor to find a wife for his son Isaac. The servant prayed that the woman who gave water to him and his camels would be God's chosen wife for Isaac (Gen. 24:10–28). The young woman whom God chose was Rebekah.

It was providence, but Rebekah still had to choose (Gen. 24:58). Like us, Rebekah had to decide on faith. She had to give up everything she knew to follow a stranger into a strange new world.

I remember sitting on the front porch of my cousin's house and saying a silent prayer. "Please let him be the one, God." I was sitting next to someone I had just met. I hoped it was my future husband. Three months later, I married that man. By God's design, grace, and protection, he has been my husband for thirty-four years. I often wonder how many people at our wedding thought, *oh, like this will last.* Well, it did last.

When you seek His will, He shows the way. But, like Rebekah, you must be willing to follow.

As you journal today, write about a decision you need to make. What uncomfortable path is God asking you to take? Will you go?

Let's Pray

Father, I know You have a plan for me. It doesn't matter my age or circumstances. If I am living, You still have work for me to do. Please help me lean into Your promises and trust You to lead me. I am willing to go. In Jesus's name, I pray. Amen.

Write It Out!

Reflect on what God is speaking to your heart today.

Date:________________________

Today I am feeling...

What one thing are you thankful for today?

Day Two

Deuteronomy 11:22 NLT
Be careful to obey all these commands I am giving you. Show love to the Lord your God by walking in his ways and holding tightly to him.

Study

Our obedience showers God's love upon us and brings us blessings, just as Rebekah's obedience brought her to Isaac. It was love at first sight, and, as Isaac was wealthy and likely handsome, life was like a fairytale come true for Rebekah. Well, except for the fact that she also struggled with infertility. However, when Isaac prayed for his wife to become pregnant, the Bible says, "The LORD answered Isaac's prayer, and Rebekah became pregnant with twins" (Genesis 25:21 NLT).

God waited for Isaac to ask. Sometimes, we lack things because we fail to ask for them. When it is God's will, He is faithful. It doesn't always happen right away, but it happens. It was twenty years before Rebekah conceived. That is a long time to wait. But in faith, Isaac showed love to God by turning to Him.

We must turn to God in prayer, but we must also remember that sometimes the answer is no. God knows what is best for us. When I was facing the fact I was going to have a special needs child, I pleaded with God. I didn't feel equipped to handle this difficulty in my life. I didn't believe my family could love a special needs child. But in God's divine wisdom, our middle child has special needs. The answer to my plea was no, but the blessings have been plentiful.

As you journal today, write about when God said, "No." Do you see the blessing in the unanswered prayer?

Let's Pray

God, I acknowledge that You know what is best for me. You know what the future holds, and in Your wisdom, I am kept safe. I give my worries to You today, and I will walk confidently as I seek wisdom in Your Word. In Jesus's name. Amen.

Write It Out!

Reflect on what God is speaking to your heart today.

Date:__________________________

Today I am feeling...

What one thing are you thankful for today?

Day Three

Romans 12:21 NIV
Do not be overcome by evil,
but overcome evil with good.

Study

If we desire to feel loved, we must go to the source. We must change our perspective and not allow the enemy to plant thoughts in our minds that make us question our position and worthiness.

Feelings are fickle. The Bible (Jer. 7:19) says, "The heart is deceitful" because when we allow our emotions to determine our feelings, the truth is elusive. When we live on emotions, it won't matter how many blessings we receive—the good will never overshadow the bad.

Rebekah finally got her wish, and now she experienced a war inside her belly. These are the first recorded twins in the Bible, and they weren't even peaceful in the womb.

I wonder if Rebekah regretted asking God why her belly had so much activity. Did she wish she had remained clueless? There are things God wants us to remain clueless about, but when He reveals things, we must open our eyes no matter how difficult the subject matter is.

The evil of human trafficking comes to my mind. It stayed hidden for years, but now God is revealing it to the world. Through movies like *Sound of Freedom*, we see the evil in this world. This factual story shines a light on what goes on under our noses daily. No, it's not comfortable to watch, but to close our eyes doesn't make it disappear. We have a responsibility to sound the alarm, and pray for God's deliverance.

As you journal today, identify ways you can show others kindness. How will you actively spread God's love?

Let's Pray

Father, it is difficult for me to look upon the evil in this world. You made me to love the light and hate darkness. I desire to be obedient to You. As I step into the role You have for me, I ask for shielding from things that might harm me. I trust You, Lord. I pray this in Jesus's name. Amen.

Write It Out!

Reflect on what God is speaking to your heart today.

Date:__________________________

Today I am feeling...

What one thing are you thankful for today?

Day Four

Colossians 3:14 ESV
And above all these put on love,
which binds everything together in perfect harmony.

Study

Do you have siblings? I have four sisters. We often fought like crazy, but we were never divided. God blessed our family with unity.

This was not true with Isaac and Rebekah's boys, Esau and Jacob. Isaac and Rebekah's house was definitely divided. And Mom and Dad chose favorites. Isaac chose Esau and Rebekah chose Jacob. Esau was prideful and wild, while Jacob was calm, cool, and collected. Their personalities were as different as the paths they chose in life. God knew this from the beginning. This wasn't just a family divided—it was a prophetic divide between good and evil and between God's people and satan's. It was a divide between love and hate.

The enemy enjoys whispering words of hate in our ears. As I type this, I'm reminded of the movie *Greater*, based on the real-life story of Brandon Burlsworth, who some consider the greatest walk-on player in college football history.[12] The movie did a great job depicting the doubt the devil puts in our thoughts. At Brandon's funeral, satan was portrayed as a bitter man who sat on a bench next to Brandon's brother, Marty. The story illustrates Marty's struggle with the loss of his brother. He contends with the devil's incessant words of doubt in God's goodness. But good always wins when we trust in God's promises.

As you journal today, write about trusting God and His loving-kindness. What is God asking you to do that is contrary to the world's standard or viewpoint?

Let's Pray

Lord, I know You don't expect me to be perfect. I am thankful You forgive our moments of doubt. Please show me Your presence daily and help me step into faith no matter the circumstances. I pray this in Jesus's name. Amen.

Write It Out!

Reflect on what God is speaking to your heart today.

Date:________________________

Today I am feeling...

What one thing are you thankful for today?

Day Five

1 John 4:17 NLT
And as we live in God, our love grows more perfect. So we will not be afraid on the day of judgment, but we can face him with confidence because we live like Jesus here in this world.

Study

Just like in the story of Esau and Jacob, God knows who will align with Him. It is always our choice, but because He knows everything, He knows how we will choose. God knows a person's heart.

You will never seek something you don't think you need. You will never find something you don't want. Likewise, when we seek for the wrong reason, we seek in vain. For God's love to grow perfect in us, we must aspire to live like Jesus. We must live for God, and throw off that fleshy desire to please the world.

Going back to the movie *Greater*, throwing off the fleshy desire to please the world is precisely what Brandon Burlsworth did. He didn't listen to the opinions of the other players. He would have quit on the first day if he had done that. Brandon wasn't naturally talented, and he wasn't athletically built. He weighed over three hundred pounds as a walk-on for the Razorbacks, but it wasn't muscle. The other players called him a nerd because he didn't drink and party like they did. It was more important for him to read his Bible. And it didn't matter that they attacked him on all fronts. He never quit. Brandon had both tenacity and a desire to please God. These qualities served him well. We can't be like Esau and sell God's love to gain the world's love.

As you journal today, write about ways God has shown you love. How can you show someone God's love today?

Let's Pray

Father, it can be easy to lash out in anger. Help me remember that Jesus showed love for those who sent Him to the cross. Please help me rest in Your love today. In Jesus's name, I pray. Amen.

Write It Out!

Reflect on what God is speaking to your heart today.

Date:________________________

Today I am feeling...

What one thing are you thankful for today?

Day Six

Dig Deeper

Read Genesis 25:19–34.

It may feel like God is punishing us when we go through trials, however the Bible tells us there will be trials. We may not understand what He asks us to do, but there is always purpose.

Abraham didn't understand why God asked him to sacrifice his only son, but he still obeyed. When Abraham obeyed, God stopped him and provided a ram. It was Abraham's obedience and trust God wanted, not his son.

That's what the Lord requires from us, also—our trust and obedience. Brandon Burlsworth had a desire to play football for the Arkansas Razorbacks. The odds were against him, and several key people along the way told him his dream was impossible. But with God, all things are possible (Matthew 19:26). Brandon chose never to quit, and God used him in mighty ways. We could all learn a lesson from Brandon.

Just this morning, as my alarm rang at 3:00 a.m. and I reluctantly climbed out of bed, tired and running on empty, I needed a Brandon reminder. As I sat wondering what to write, I thought, *if this is God's will, isn't it supposed to be easy*? Had I misunderstood God? I opened my Bible Hub app, and this is the verse I read: "When you ask, you must believe and not doubt, because the one who doubts is like a wave of the sea, blown and tossed by the wind. That person should not expect to receive anything from the Lord. Such a person is double-minded and unstable in all they do" (James 1:6–8 NIV). Mic drop!

As you journal today, ask God to help you believe in what He's asking you to do. What challenging thing are you doing for His glory?

Let's Pray

Lord, this life is never easy, and when we choose You above everything else, it can seem harder. Please strengthen me and give me the tenacity to stay in the fight for Your glory, not mine. In Jesus's name. Amen.

Write It Out!

Reflect on what God is speaking to your heart today.

Date:__________________________

Today I am feeling...

What one thing are you thankful for today?

Day Seven

Today is a day to rest and reflect. This is a great day to complete the End of Week Goal Tracker and see your progress. Use the section below for sermon notes, rest in the Lord, and enjoy your family.

Write It Out!

Reflect on what God is speaking to your heart today.

Date:______________________

Sermon Notes:

Prayer Journal

What are you praying for? Write your prayers here. As your prayers are answered, jot down the day and how God answered. Was it what you prayed for or something better?

I am praying that God will…	Date	God answered by…

Who will you pray for this week?

Person/Organization:

Need:

Person/Organization:

Need:

"God is love. He didn't need us.
But he wanted us. And that is the
most amazing thing."

—Rick Warren

Week Seven

Day One

John 15:9 NKJV
As the Father loved Me,
I also have loved you; abide in My love.

Study

Jacob went to herd sheep for Laban in Haran. He made a deal to work for seven years in exchange for Laban's daughter, Rachel. The Bible says Jacob loved Rachel so much that the seven years of work seemed like only a few days (Gen. 29:20). When the time came, Jacob reminded Laban of the deal, and arrangements were made. However, Laban put Rachel's older sister, Leah, in her place. The Bible doesn't tell us if a rivalry between the two sisters existed before this event, but we know how deep it was after. But God uses broken people.

We are all broken, but thankfully, the Lord still has a purpose for each of us. We get mad at God and blame Him for things we don't like about our lives or circumstances, while He leads us where He wants us.

One of my husband's and my favorite things to do is watch *Anne of Green Gables.* When I think of how people blame God for life circumstances, I think of Anne. She says someone told her God made her hair red on purpose. Without emotion, she adds, "I haven't liked Him since." That's what we often do. When we don't like something about our life, we choose to blame God. We take a feature that makes us unique and special, and we make it a curse.

We get so fixated on a perceived flaw that we can't move forward until it is "fixed." We place ourselves in a prison of condemnation.

As you journal today, write about something you don't like about yourself. End your journaling with this sentence: "My perceived flaws don't determine my worth. I am perfect and priceless to God."

Let's Pray

Father, I know in Your eyes I am priceless. Please help me see myself the way You see me. Because of Jesus, I am perfect. Amen.

Write It Out!

Reflect on what God is speaking to your heart today.

Date:________________________

Today I am feeling...

What one thing are you thankful for today?

Day Two

1 Corinthians 16:14 NKJV
Let all that you do be done with love.

Study

The love between Rachel and Leah was strained from the beginning. Rachel's looks and the love Jacob had for her overshadowed Leah and created a huge divide. But God leveled the playing field. The Bible says, "When the LORD saw that Leah was unloved, he enabled her to have children, but Rachel could not conceive" (Genesis 29:31 NLT).

God loved both Leah and Rachel. There was a trial in their lives to strengthen them. We are made perfect in our weakness (2 Cor. 12:9). No matter what we face, the battle is won or lost in our minds. It doesn't matter what we are fighting for—if the enemy has defeated us with our thoughts, the chances of victory are slim to none. This is why it is vital to know our identity and do everything with love. The more we love, the more we feel loved.

When we wrap our hands around the neck of our enemies in unforgiveness, they don't feel the grip. We remain focused on the offense as they walk around unhindered by our anger. A scene from the movie *Ghost* comes to mind. In this nineties movie, the main character, Sam Wheat, was murdered and walks around as a ghost. He knows who shot him, and he tries to fight back and get revenge. But his efforts are all in vain. We see Sam punching with all his might, and the murderer walks around unfazed. Sam's attacks don't affect him because he can't see Sam or feel his assault. Sam is only wearing himself out.

There is freedom in surrender. As you journal today, write about feelings you need to surrender to God.

Let's Pray

Lord, I know I have carried around feelings of unforgiveness. Please help me release these feelings to You and be free from this bondage. In Jesus's name. Amen.

Write It Out

Reflect on what God is speaking to your heart today.

Date:__________________________

Today I am feeling...

What one thing are you thankful for today?

Day Three

2 Thessalonians 3:5 NKJV
Now may the Lord direct your hearts into the love of God and into the patience of Christ.

Study

When I wrote about Rachel in my book *Gathering the Wayward Heart*, I focused on the beautiful love story about how Jacob worked to marry Rachel. He was willing to work fourteen years for the girl he loved.

Rachel may have been physically beautiful, but, as my mom used to say, beauty is only skin deep. Rachel was a controlling drama queen. She decided who did what and when. Can you imagine how annoyed she was at her infertility?

We have no control in these situations, but like Rachel, we have God. Our help comes from the Lord (Psalm 121:2). However, some people see God as their enemy when He doesn't "deliver."

We will never have peace when we see God as our enemy and not our helper. Likewise, we will never feel loved when we look to the world for validation.

Hope Lives is a movie that delves into the lives of six teenagers who experience bullying in school. One of the girls, Maria, seems to have it all. She has physical beauty, is popular, and has a large social media following. On the outside, she has it all together. However, her mother struggles with alcohol, her father is in prison, and she feels unloved. The "love" she receives from the world is fleeting and fickle.

As you journal, write about the love God has shown you. Where are you searching for love? Is your cup filled?

Let's Pray

Father, please help me see Your love daily. Help me remember that I will only feel loved when I am confident in Your love. In Jesus's name, I pray. Amen.

Write It Out!

Reflect on what God is speaking to your heart today.

Date:________________________

Today I am feeling...

What one thing are you thankful for today?

Day Four

Ephesians 3:17 NLT
Then Christ will make his home in your hearts as you trust in him. Your roots will grow down into God's love and keep you strong.

Study

We likely all know someone who loves themselves so much they cannot give love to others. They haven't allowed Christ to fill their heart with love, and they still live in a "me" world. We all struggle with this to some degree, especially when we are younger, but if left unchecked, it only worsens. The person who refuses to let Christ's love into their heart doesn't grow deep roots. They have no foundation, and when things don't go their way, they fearfully grab for control.

That is where we find Rachel in Genesis 30:14–16. She is clutching for control and leveraging her position as the favorite wife to get what she wants. It is all a game devised by satan. We leverage what we have to gain that one step forward, thinking, *if I can get this one thing, I will be happy.* But when we get there, we are still unhappy. Until we fill that God-shaped hole deep in our souls, nothing will ever be enough. We will never feel like we are enough. And we will never feel loved.

God is love, and no one will satisfy our need for love except Him. We can't get something from the world that doesn't exist in the world. True love comes from God. When we read His Word, His love letter to us, we are filled with His love.

As you journal today, describe what perfect love looks like to you. In what ways do you feel unloved today?

Let's Pray

Father, I know that perfect love doesn't exist without you. I feel loved in new relationships, but that feeling always fades with time. Please help me be filled with Your love as I seek You and read Your Word. Help me throw off the cloak of doubt the world has placed over me and seek only You. I pray this in Jesus's name. Amen.

Write It Out!

Reflect on what God is speaking to your heart today.

Date:________________________

Today I am feeling...

What one thing are you thankful for today?

Day Five

Ephesians 3:18 NLT
And may you have the power to understand, as all God's people should, how wide, how long, how high, and how deep his love is.

Study

Rachel was in emotional turmoil when she couldn't have children. She looked at her sister, who was having babies left and right, and it infuriated her. It was the only way she felt second to her sister. So, when Leah's son brought her mandrakes, which were said to help with infertility, Rachel pounced. In Genesis 30:14–16, we get a clear picture of the control Rachel had. She could bargain with Jacob's sleeping arrangements. Rachel was still relying on her ability and determination. But even with all that control, she was still subject to God's will. The Lord determined what Rachel received.

It is amazing that the Lord has a plan for each of us. Just think about it for one minute. God, who controls everything in this universe, has a plan for you. He knows you by name, and He sees your struggles.

In the movie *Hope Lives*, the man who steps into the school to teach the class about bullying is no stranger to its effects. His daughter died while being bullied. It was a tragic, life-altering event. But it made him seek a new lifestyle and placed him in the lives of children who needed his guidance. In his quest for understanding and healing, God used him to help and heal others. What event from your past is God asking you to use to help others?

As you journal today, ask God to reveal something that needs healing in your life. Ask Him to show you how to use your healed pain to help others.

Let's Pray

Father, I know You love me, and I trust in Your healing. Please help me release the hurt I need to, and help me use my scars to help others. I pray this in Jesus's name. Amen.

Write It Out!

Reflect on what God is speaking to your heart today.

Date:__________________________

Today I am feeling...

What one thing are you thankful for today?

Day Six

Dig Deeper

Read Genesis 31:1–21.

When we feel unworthy, we doubt God's redeeming grace and further separate ourselves from His love. Many of us are like Rachel, always clutching and grasping for more. Even though God "remembered Rachel's plight" and gave her a son (Gen. 30:22), she wasn't happy. She wanted bigger and better. She looked down at the face of her newborn child and immediately wanted another son (Gen. 30:24).

How often do we do that? We receive a blessing, experience tremendous joy, and then turn to God and say, "More, please." We do that when we need others' love and approval to validate us. We turn to other sinful people and expect them to make us feel whole and worthy, but it's impossible because no person will ever be able to give us enough.

In the movie *Hope Lives*, several characters futilely sought love and validation from the world. Wanda struggled with her weight. She tried her best to be invisible, but everyone noticed her when she showed up late to class. One of her biggest problems wasn't her weight—it was the perception she had about herself. She saw herself through society's eyes, not God's. Losing the weight may have helped for a moment, but it wouldn't have been the solution. She wouldn't be free until she saw herself as God saw her.

As you journal today, compare society's vision of who you are to God's. How do you see yourself? Is it through God's eyes or the world's?

Let's Pray

Father, I know my vision is warped when I look at myself in the mirror. I tend to judge myself on society's standards, not Yours. Help me shed the labels the world has placed on me and see myself as You do. I pray this in Jesus's name. Amen.

Write It Out!

Reflect on what God is speaking to your heart today.

Date:_______________________

Today I am feeling...

What one thing are you thankful for today?

Day Seven

Today is a day to rest and reflect. This is a great day to complete the End of Week Goal Tracker and see your progress. Use the section below for sermon notes, rest in the Lord, and enjoy your family.

Write It Out!

Reflect on what God is speaking to your heart today.

Date:______________________

Sermon Notes:

Prayer Journal

What are you praying for? Write your prayers here. As your prayers are answered, jot down the day and how God answered. Was it what you prayed for or something better?

I am praying that God will…	Date	God answered by…

Who will you pray for this week?

Person/Organization:

Need:

Person/Organization:

Need:

"God proved His love on the Cross. When Christ hung, and bled, and died, it was God saying to the world, 'I love you.'"

— Billy Graham

Week Eight

Day One

Ephesians 3:19 NLT
May you experience the love of Christ,
though it is too great to understand fully.
Then you will be made complete with all the
fullness of life and power that comes from God.

Study

How do we fully understand and experience the love of Christ? When we live in a battle-torn world and face opposition daily, how can we have confidence that God is in control? When we are distant from God, we can't. It is impossible to see His footprints in our lives when we don't draw close to Him daily.

Hannah, like most of the women we studied, was barren. She wanted desperately to have a child. But unlike others, she didn't grasp for control—she sought God. Hannah's story reminds us of God's love and power. She approached her trouble with humble surrender. It was God's will, not hers.

In my book, *Gathering the Wayward Heart,* I write about a time when I was desperately trying to change our circumstances regarding our living situation. Everything was set in motion. We were approved for the financing and chose a house, but it still wouldn't close. The loan officer couldn't explain why. I was frustrated, and like Rachel, I felt like I would die if I didn't get what I wanted. We didn't see the reason until we looked back at the situation. God had a better house, property, and plan for our lives. My way would have ruined God's best for us.

As you journal today, write about the blessings you received from unanswered prayers. On a Post-it note, write the following sentence and place it on your mirror: I am fully loved by Christ (Romans 8:37).

Let's Pray

Lord, I know when You close a door there is a reason. I know You have a better plan and greater blessings for me. I want to live in Your will, not mine. In Jesus's name, I pray. Amen.

Write It Out!

Reflect on what God is speaking to your heart today.

Date:________________________

Today I am feeling...

What one thing are you thankful for today?

Day Two

1 John 4:10 NLT
This is real love—not that we loved God, but that he loved us and sent his Son as a sacrifice to take away our sins.

Study

Hannah knew that Peninnah didn't like her. 1 Samuel 1:7 NIV says, "Her rival provoked her till she wept and would not eat." But Peninnah's behavior was reflective of herself not Hannah. Her behavior came from feeling unloved. She provided their husband Elkanah with plenty of children. In her mind, she was the better wife, but she wasn't the loved wife. Just like some of us, she sought love from the wrong place.

Hannah was the one who had Elkanah's heart. He loved her, but she still felt empty without a child. The difference between Hannah and Rachel is Hannah sought God's love and His will. She went to the source for both, and then she had hope (1 Samuel 1:18).

How often do we go to the foot of the cross, lay our burden down, and walk away with unbelief? Unfortunately, I must raise my hand to that. When I had little to no fellowship with the Lord, I had little faith in Him. With arrogance, I attempted to kick down the doors He closed. I believed I knew what was best. And where did that leave me? It left me broken. I was in a broken marriage, a broken family, and a broken life. God rebuilt everything. When we approach the throne of God, we must have unwavering faith.

When you journal today, thank God for rebuilding your life. On a Post-it note, write the following sentence and place it on your mirror: "I am chosen by God" (John 15:16).

Let's Pray

Thank you, Father, for the places You restore in my life. I pray for Your continued healing. Please pick up the broken pieces in my life and put them back together. Thank You for choosing me. I pray this in Jesus's name. Amen.

Write It Out!

Reflect on what God is speaking to your heart today.

Date:__________________________

Today I am feeling...

What one thing are you thankful for today?

Day Three

Romans 5:5 NIV
And hope does not put us to shame,
because God's love has been poured out
into our hearts through the Holy Spirit,
who has been given to us.

Study

Hannah's attitude changed instantly because she had faith in God. She still had to go home and face Peninnah and wait to find out if she would have a child, but she did all of it with an uplifted spirit. The Bible says that when we are among the living, we still have hope. It doesn't matter what past mistakes you have made or your circumstances. There is always hope. Like Hannah, you can lay your burdens down and walk away with the hope that comes from trusting in the Lord.

I remember when I walked away from the life I lived as a reckless teen. I felt like I was searching for love my whole life. But the fact was, I had love and refused to recognize it. People around me cared for me, and I passed that off as nothing. It wasn't the filling love I was searching for. I always needed more.

We walk around as broken vessels. We are cracked, so the love others pour into us runs out. That's why we need constant filling. God's love is poured into us, but if we don't believe He loves us, it runs out. The greatest crack in my vessel was caused by needing to be filled but not seeking to fill others.

As you journal today, reflect on what's hard to release to God (e.g., pride, money, time). On a Post-it note, write the following sentence and place it on your mirror: "I am filled with God's love" (Romans 5:5).

Let's Pray

Father, I know I'm still holding onto hurt. I desire to live in Your perfect love—not the shallow fleeting love of the world, but Your true love. Please help me surrender all to You. I pray this in Jesus's name. Amen.

Write It Out!

Reflect on what God is speaking to your heart today.

Date:________________________

Today I am feeling...

What one thing are you thankful for today?

Day Four

1 John 4:9 NLT
God showed how much he loved us by sending his one and only Son into the world so that we might have eternal life through him.

Study

Relationship, not religion, is the key to feeling loved and at peace. Hannah entered the house of God and prayed intently. It was just her and God during that moment.

Hannah promised to give the one thing she desired most back to God. That meant before her son was five, she promised to take him to live in the tabernacle and only see him once a year. It must have been a difficult promise to keep. But Hannah was good to her word, and God blessed her with many more children.

How often do people promise the moon when they want something and forget the vow when they receive it? So many today turn to God in trouble and then rob Him of the credit. They think it was luck that shined upon them. We need to see God's hand in everything.

I remember walking out of a store, and a man walked up behind me so close it was uncomfortable. I thought he planned to rob me, and I said a silent prayer. After that prayer, he rushed past me and almost knocked into me. I think he was spooked by people who had climbed out of a pickup in front of us. That's how God protects.

As you journal today, write about God's protection. On a Post-it note, write the following sentence and place it on your mirror: "I am a warrior through Christ who loves me" (Rom. 8:37).

Let's Pray

Father, I am so thankful for the protection You give me daily. I don't want to go through life on autopilot and not acknowledge the war I cannot see. There is a battle going on around me right now and I thank You for keeping me safe. In Jesus's name. Amen.

Write It Out!

Reflect on what God is speaking to your heart today.

Date:________________________

Today I am feeling...

What one thing are you thankful for today?

Day Five

Romans 5:8 ESV
But God shows his love for us in that while we were still sinners, Christ died for us.

Study

Most people go through their days without thinking about God or what He has done. Christ willingly died so we could spend eternity with Him in heaven. This is the utmost in love. As people insulted and spat at Him, He said, "Father, forgive them because they don't know what they are doing" (Luke 23:34 NLT). This is the kind of love He gives us.

To fully embrace love, we must actively give love. Hannah embraced God's love toward her and then returned it to Him through sacrifice. True love is a self-sacrifice. It doesn't mean we let someone abuse us, but it does mean we give more than we get. It means we sometimes must give something we love back to God.

In the movie *Hope Lives*, Maria's perspective changed when she looked at life through a different lens. She extended compassion to her mother instead of insults and judgment. Because she could do that, she helped change the lives of those around her. Her mother took steps to get away from alcohol.

When we react with love in all situations, it is like a domino effect. Proverbs 15:1 NIV says, "A gentle answer turns away wrath, but a harsh word stirs up anger." Our words matter, and selfless love goes a long way to mend a hurting heart.

As you journal today, reflect on your relationship with those around you. On a Post-it note, write the following sentence and place it on your mirror: "I am a child of God" (John 1:12).

Let's Pray

Father, please help me approach those You have placed in my life with increased love and kindness. I may not always agree, and relationships are sometimes strained, but You have placed them in my life to love. Help me love them completely. In Jesus's name. Amen.

Write It Out!

Reflect on what God is speaking to your heart today.

Date:__________________________

Today I am feeling...

What one thing are you thankful for today?

Day Six

Dig Deeper

Read 1 Samuel 1:24–28 and 1 Samuel 2:1–11 and 18–21.

Do you see how Hannah rejoiced? She didn't get everything her way, but God answered her prayer and then gave her more than she asked for. God had a huge purpose for Samuel. When we pray for God's will upon our lives, we receive more than we ask for. God's plan for your life is the perfect plan. But don't fall into the trap of thinking life will be perfect and easy.

In the movie *Pilgrim's Progress*, when Christian started his journey, Obstinate and Pliable cut him off. They attempted to change his mind about following Christ. When Christian told them the promise of heaven, Obstinate wanted no part of it. He was unwilling to leave the comforts of his life, no matter the promises of a better one. Pliable got excited and wanted to get there as soon as possible. Rushing ahead, they both fell into the muddy swamp of despair. Pulling himself up on the bank, Pliable said, "If this is what it's like to follow you in the beginning, how could it possibly be any better in the end?" Pliable was following for the wrong reasons.

Read Genesis 37:18–28. Through Joseph, God rescued His people. But we can't leave God out of the victory celebration. It's God's work. We are just the vessel He uses to accomplish it.

As you journal today, lay your worries before God, and ask for His blessings and intervention in your life. On a Post-it note, write the following sentence and place it on your mirror: "I am called to complete God's plan" (Romans 8:28).

Let's Pray

Father, I know I can trust You in every trial. You are working for me, and I believe in Your promises. Please help me in every circumstance. I pray this in Jesus's name. Amen.

Write It Out!

Reflect on what God is speaking to your heart today.

Date:________________________

Today I am feeling...

What one thing are you thankful for today?

Day Seven

Today is a day to rest and reflect. This is a great day to complete the End of Week Goal Tracker and see your progress. Use the section below for sermon notes, rest in the Lord, and enjoy your family.

Write It Out!

Reflect on what God is speaking to your heart today.

Date:______________________

Sermon Notes:

Prayer Journal

What are you praying for? Write your prayers here. As your prayers are answered, jot down the day and how God answered. Was it what you prayed for or something better?

I am praying that God will…	Date	God answered by…

Who will you pray for this week?

Person/Organization:

Need:

Person/Organization:

Need:

"There is no pit so deep, that God's love is not deeper still."

— Corrie Ten Boom

Week Nine

Day One

1 John 3:1 ESV
See what kind of love the Father has given to us, that we should be called children of God; and so we are. The reason why the world does not know us is that it did not know him.

Study

In these next few weeks, we will look at four women. They are all different in many ways, but they have one thing in common. These four women all walked with the living God. And while we would like to think that if we walked with God Himself, we would be better off, these women show us that even they faltered at times.

One of these women lived life in reverse. Eve was the only woman to walk this earth who lived during a period of perfection. Unlike those who strive to be perfect in Christ, Eve had it and threw it all away. The other three women walked with Jesus. Mary, the mother of Jesus, Mary of Bethany, and Martha.

These women show us that everyone's journey is difficult. We all have doubts, fears, and frustrations. None of these women were without sin. We all need a Savior. Eve helped bring sin into the world, and we all fall victim to it. Even Mary, Jesus's mother, needed a Savior (Romans 3:23). But God is with us every step.

As you journal today, reflect on the victory you have in Christ. How have you seen victory in your life, and what are you hoping for in the future? On a Post-it note, write the following sentence and place it on your mirror: "I am valuable" (John 15:16).

Let's Pray

Father, You are my ultimate victory. Thank You for salvation. I know it doesn't matter how fearful things seem because You are always in control. You will never let my enemies win against me. Thank You for that protection. In Jesus's name, I pray. Amen.

Write It Out!

Reflect on what God is speaking to your heart today.

Date:__________________________

Today I am feeling...

What one thing are you thankful for today?

Day Two

Psalm 89:1 NLT
I will sing of the Lord's unfailing love forever!
Young and old will hear of your faithfulness.

Study

We all have a new identity in Christ, but we often stumble around in the past, refusing to cast off the burdens we place upon ourselves. We become people who are bound by legalism. That's what "religion" does. Religion heaps upon us various rules and goals that must be obtained before someone is free. But that is not meant for those who know Christ. Jesus took the rules and regulations upon Himself and broke the chains of legalism. On your journey, you will still fail, but that doesn't mean you are a failure.

In the movie *The Case for Christ*, which is Lee Strobel's story, his wife Leslie came to know Christ before he did. If she had half-heartedly embraced the message of salvation, she could have continued to live peacefully in a marriage with a nonbeliever. But she couldn't do that. The news was too valuable to keep hidden—her joy was too great.

Their marriage was turned upside down and in constant turmoil. Determined to burst the bubble she was living in, Lee set out to disprove the Bible and the resurrection of Christ. To his surprise, he found it was impossible. Anytime someone tries to disprove the Bible, they come to Christ. Isn't that an amazing consequence?

As you journal today, be inspired by the beauty of coming to Christ. Recall your salvation or remember when a friend or loved one was saved. On a Post-it note, write the following sentence and place it on your mirror: "I am a healed through Christ" (1 Pet. 2:24).

Let's Pray

Father, I pray for those who don't know you. You are the Light of the world, and they are stumbling around in darkness with no hope. It's not always easy to give them grace when they lash out, but please help me do it. I pray in Jesus's name. Amen.

Write It Out!

Reflect on what God is speaking to your heart today.

Date:________________________

Today I am feeling...

What one thing are you thankful for today?

Day Three

Proverbs 10:12 NIV
Hatred stirs up conflict,
but love covers over all wrongs.

Study

Eve is the perfect example of not knowing what we have until it's gone. Wow, when I think about the beginning days of Eve, I am struck with the instant pain she must have felt after she took that bite. As the enemy filled her head with lies, her thoughts were spinning. I imagine him pointing out imaginary flaws in Adam, herself, and her environment. Everything was perfect, but he made her want more.

How often does he do that with us? He is a master at making us double-minded. He tries to mold our perspective, just as he did Eve's. And that ol' devil pulls out all the stops. A friend makes a harmless comment, or an unsuspecting husband doesn't think before he speaks, and the enemy uses it. If we don't recognize it as a lie from the pit of hell, it can ruin relationships. Satan reminds us about everything we believe the world thinks of us. He plays on your past hurt and misunderstanding.

We also must remember that others are listening to the enemy whispering in their ears. That husband, mother, or friend who is difficult to love is also under attack. If they are lost, think of how hopeless they feel, and unfortunately, all they know to do is lash out. If you are shining a light and they love the darkness, you will be the target. It isn't about you, it's about them and God.

As you journal today, reflect on the light of truth. How do you want others to see you? On a Post-it note, write the following sentence and place it on your mirror: "I am a light in a dark world" (Matt. 5:14).

Let's Pray

Father, please help me remember that people aren't against me. They live without hope. Help me have compassion for them. And help me continue to shine Your light. In Jesus's name, I pray. Amen.

Write It Out!

Reflect on what God is speaking to your heart today.

Date:__________________________

Today I am feeling...

What one thing are you thankful for today?

Day Four

Psalm 51:1 NLT
Have mercy on me, O God,
because of your unfailing love.
Because of your great compassion,
blot out the stain of my sins.

Study

We tend to think God can't see past our flaws, especially when we are newly saved. Like the character named Christian in *Pilgrim's Progress*, we walk around with our burdens strapped to our backs. We no longer want them, but we don't know how to rid ourselves of them.

When we allow others to tell us who we are, we turn our backs on what Christ did on the cross. When we live in that identity, we don't embrace the victory of the cross. Don't leave Jesus on the cross. The victory is in His defeating death. It is in the resurrection.

Can you imagine what would have happened if Mary, the mother of Jesus, weighed out the thoughts of others when the angel appeared to her? Now, it's not like the angel appeared to the world and said, "Listen up, world. This woman will carry God's Son, so don't judge her." No, she needed to trust God to pave the way, and He did.

God has a plan for you, also. As you seek His will and follow His plan, you must drown out the voices of the world and focus on God's voice. Don't let that ol' devil sneak in and steal your joy. Don't let him convince you that you are unloved.

As you journal today, reflect on the sacrifice Christ made for you. Picture Him on the cross, but, more importantly, in His resurrected glory. On a Post-it note, write the following sentence and place it on your mirror: "I am free in Christ" (Gal. 4:7).

Let's Pray

Lord, thank You for sending Your Son, and thank You, Jesus, for dying for me. Please keep me from allowing the voices of the world to drown out the only voice that matters—Yours. In Jesus's name. Amen.

Write It Out

Reflect on what God is speaking to your heart today.

Date:________________________

Today I am feeling...

What one thing are you thankful for today?

Day Five

John 17:23 NLT
I am in them and you are in me. May they experience such perfect unity that the world will know that you sent me and that you love them as much as you love me.

Study

Anyone who belongs to Christ has become a new person. The old life is gone; a new life has begun!" (2 Cor. 5:17). The word "new" translated in this verse is *kainos*, which means "something just made that's unlike anything else in existence."[13] So, you are made new, and you are unique.

When Mary of Bethany sat at the feet of Jesus, intently listening to His teaching, Jesus commented that Mary discovered the one thing on which she should be focused. Mary was listening and learning. She wasn't distracted by the world.

Distractions lead us down the wrong road and make us chase after the wrong things. The enemy knows the traps we will likely fall into. A great example from *Pilgrim's Progress* is when Flatterer convinces Christian and Hopeful to follow the wrong path. The more they listen to his praise, the further they veer off course and find themselves bragging. Before they realize what is happening, they are caught in a trap.

When we focus on the wrong things, we miss what we are supposed to be. The enemy will make your true identity appear to be an ever-moving target, but it's not. If we embraced that truth, there would be no more jealousy or bitter competition among God's people. A child of the King doesn't have to fight for scraps.

As you journal today, write about the path you are on and how you plan to stay on course. On a Post-it note, write the following sentence and place it on your mirror: "I am unique in Christ" (2 Cor. 5:17).

Let's Pray

Father, help me stay on the path You set before me. Help me not veer to the left or to the right. Keep me on course as I run this race of life. In Jesus's name, I pray. Amen.

Write It Out!

Reflect on what God is speaking to your heart today.

Date:________________________

Today I am feeling...

What one thing are you thankful for today?

Day Six

Dig Deeper

Read John 10:1–21.

The only way to know God is to read His Word. John 10:27 NLT says, "My sheep listen to my voice; I know them, and they follow me." People who are not saved don't know God's voice.

I heard someone say, "I am a good person. I can't imagine God wouldn't allow good people into heaven." So, I had to pull out some Ray Comfort. I replied, "Imagine if someone raped and brutally murdered your wife. At the trial, they stood before the judge and said, 'Yes, judge, I did those things, but other than this one act, I am a good person. I feed the homeless, and I give to charity. Would you expect the judge to sentence him on the good things he had done or on murdering your wife?" Without thinking, he said, "Murdering my wife, of course."

"God doesn't see sin from small to big," I continued. "Sin is sin. As a matter of fact, lying and murder are mentioned in the same sentence. To God, they are equally offensive. So, if you would expect an earthly judge to sentence justly, then God, who is the perfect judge, will sentence justly." I added one more thought. "The Bible says that if we have been angry with someone, we have murdered them in our heart, so we are all murderers."

Plant the seed and let God water it. It's not our job to drag people into heaven. God alone knows the seeds to water.

As you journal today, write about ways you can plant seeds of salvation. On a Post-it note, write the following sentence and place it on your mirror: "I am called" (1 Thess. 5:24).

Let's Pray

Father, You are the God of salvation. I don't know who will come and who will reject, but You do. Please give me opportunities to plant seeds as I go through this day. I trust You, and I want You to use me. In Jesus's name, I pray. Amen.

Write It Out!

Reflect on what God is speaking to your heart today.

Date:__________________________

Today I am feeling...

What one thing are you thankful for today?

Day Seven

Today is a day to rest and reflect. This is a great day to complete the End of Week Goal Tracker and see your progress. Use the section below for sermon notes, rest in the Lord, and enjoy your family.

Write It Out!

Reflect on what God is speaking to your heart today.

Date:______________________

Sermon Notes:

Prayer Journal

What are you praying for? Write your prayers here. As your prayers are answered, jot down the day and how God answered. Was it what you prayed for or something better?

I am praying that God will…	Date	God answered by…

Who will you pray for this week?

Person/Organization:

Need:

Person/Organization:

Need:

"He loved us not because we are lovable, but because He is love."

—C.S. Lewis

Week Ten

Day One

John 3:16 NIV
For God so loved the world that he gave his one and only Son, that whoever believes in him shall not perish but have eternal life.

Study

In *Control Girl*, Shannon Popkin points out something I'd never thought of before. Why did God put the tree with the forbidden fruit in the middle of the garden (Gen. 3:3)?

The temptation to go against God's command was front and center. But why? Well, Shannon shared wise insight on that. While the tree and fruit were undisturbed, it showed that Adam and Eve trusted God's plan and control over their lives. They had a perfect life—all they had to do was live in paradise and love God. But the human heart is wicked (Jer. 17:9). The enemy played on Eve's desires and dangled the fruit before her, saying, "You will be like God, knowing good and evil" (Gen. 3:5 ESV). So, Adam and Eve took a bite.

But how can this all be a part of God's plan? Simple—it's called free will. We get to choose. Lee Strobel, who wrote *The Case For Christ*, tells an amazing story about a man behind a desk. I love his story about the man behind the desk who overheard him inviting an atheist friend to his church's Easter service.[14] The atheist friend rejected the invitation, but that conversation led the man behind the desk, his wife, and their teenage son to Christ.

As you journal today, think about the man behind the desk. Write about how you are fulfilling your purpose by planting seeds of salvation and love. On a Post-it note, write the following sentence and place it on your mirror: "I am appointed" (John 15:16).

Let's Pray

Father, it isn't always comfortable to share Your love with nonbelievers. Please give me the strength and courage to share Your Word with those who need to hear it. I pray this in Jesus's name. Amen.

Write It Out!

Reflect on what God is speaking to your heart today.

Date:__________________________

Today I am feeling...

What one thing are you thankful for today?

Day Two

Romans 8:38–39 NIV

. . . neither death nor life, neither angels nor demons, neither the present nor the fture, nor any powers, neither height nor depth, nor anything else inall creation, will be able to separate us from the love of God that is in Christ Jesus our Lord.

Study

Martha fell into the perfection trap as she attempted to be the perfect hostess. When she looked over at Mary sitting around doing nothing, it frustrated her (Luke 10:40). Martha missed the point. It didn't have to be perfect. When we focus on perfection, we try to turn the praise toward ourselves.

I work hard at overcoming my Martha perfectionism. I throw an annual Easter party for my extended family. The first year was just a haphazard, "Hey, let's have an Easter party." But I upped my game the second year with a scavenger hunt for the kids. Then it became, in my mind anyway, that every year must be better than the last. You can see how it could quickly get out of hand.

I didn't give up on the scavenger hunt, and every year, it became increasingly difficult to write new clues and find new hiding places. It had to be perfect, after all. But I finally realized that the kids had just as much fun, if not more, playing on the playground. The scavenger hunt had become more of a must-do task than a fun activity. Wow, my life is easier without that scavenger hunt.

As you journal today, think of something you are trying to make perfect. How can you change it to make your life easier and glorify God? On a Post-it note, write the following sentence and place it on your mirror: "I am already perfect in Christ" (1 Peter 1:19).

Let's Pray

Father, help me accept the fact that Jesus was the only perfect One to walk this planet. Please release me from the trap of my perfectionism and worry about others' opinions. I want to live freely in Your love. I pray this in Jesus's name. Amen.

Write It Out

Reflect on what God is speaking to your heart today.

Date:__________________________

Today I am feeling...

What one thing are you thankful for today?

Day Three

1 John 4:11 NLT
Dear friends, since God loved us that much,
we surely ought to love each other.

Study

In your pursuit of showing God's love, how has the enemy made you envy others? When a person starts pursuing God's plan, it can be easy to fall into the comparison trap. You look at someone with a similar purpose to yours, and it looks like they are knocking it out of the park. God has a plan for you—you don't have to share it with anyone else. We should encourage rather than discourage one another.

Martha and Mary of Bethany had the living God in their living room. Both women reacted opposite to each other. Mary chose to sit intently at the feet of Jesus, while Martha chose to be busy. When Martha looked at Mary sitting there doing nothing, the envy monster took hold. Why should Mary rest while she worked? But Martha was trying to go above and beyond.

I started my Easter parties the same way. It wasn't enough to have a fun get-together where everyone sat and enjoyed the day. Sometimes, I would stop and think, I didn't sit and visit with anyone today. I missed my party by being a Martha.

When we logically stop and look at things we get spun up about in our lives, we need to ask this question, "Does it really matter?" Does it matter if everything isn't perfect? No, it doesn't matter. So, don't miss the important moments in your life over things that don't matter.

As you journal today, write about things you stress over. Do they really matter? On a Post-it note, write the following sentence and place it on your mirror: "I am at peace because of God" (Psalm 4:8).

Let's Pray

Father, please help me recognize the trap of perfection and stop worrying about others' opinions. Help me rest in the assurance of Your love and protection. In Jesus's name. Amen.

Write It Out!

Reflect on what God is speaking to your heart today.

Date:____________________________

Today I am feeling...

What one thing are you thankful for today?

Day Four

1 John 4:12 NLT
But if we love each other, God lives in us,
and his love is brought to full expression in us.

Study

In our pursuit of showing God's love, the enemy tries to bind us with fear. Can you imagine the fear Martha and Mary felt when they knew their brother Lazarus was dead? Jesus waited two days after being told Lazarus was ill before heading to Judea (John 11:6). When Jesus arrived, Lazarus was dead. There seemed to be no hope.

But Martha met Jesus with great faith. She said something to the effect of, "If You had been here this never would have happened," and then added, "I know You can fix this." And she was right. And Mary ran to weep in the arms of Jesus. Like these ladies, we need to have unwavering faith and rest in the arms of Jesus.

I mentioned the movie *Coat of Many Colors* earlier in this book. The family grieved deeply over the loss of a precious child, and Dolly blamed God. Dolly's mom went into a state of depression, but coming out of that state, she started singing and sewing again. When Dolly asked why, her mother said something very profound. "Truth is he was never mine, and he was never yours." Dolly's mom had visions that she was going to lose the baby. When Dolly found out, she said, "If I had known, I wouldn't have loved him." Her mom replied, "Don't ever wish you hadn't loved. There is nothing on this earth more powerful than love. It's stronger than death."

As you journal today, think of the power of God's love in your life. On a Post-it note, write the following sentence and place it on your mirror: "I know real love because I am loved by God" (1 John 4:10).

Let's Pray

Father, thank You for the love You shower on my life daily. Please help me see my trials through Your eyes. I trust You, Lord. In Jesus's name, I pray. Amen.

Write It Out

Reflect on what God is speaking to your heart today.

Date:________________________

Today I am feeling...

What one thing are you thankful for today?

Day Five

Isaiah 63:9 NLT
In his love and mercy he redeemed them.
He lifted them up and carried them
through all the years.

Study

Jesus redeemed us, but we can still get stuck in the past. Imagine how Adam and Eve must have felt when the two hung their heads in shame as they were kicked out of the Garden of Eden. Adam and Eve lived a future they wished they could forget. The couple was kicked out of an exclusive club, and no matter how hard the two knocked, they would never get back in.

It reminds me of a *Frasier* episode when Frasier and his brother Niles accidentally received a neighbor's day pass to an exclusive spa. Under a false name, Frasier and Niles gained access to the basic spa amenities, which were wonderful, but the two kept finding more exclusive areas of the spa: a silver door, a gold door, and finally, a platinum door. Every time the brothers were barred from going through a door, they determined how to get through to the more exclusive area.

Wrapped in seaweed, the two fought their way through the final exclusive door which slammed and locked. Blinded by bright light, their eyes slowly adjusted—the two realized they were outside next to the trash cans. There the brothers stood, wrapped in seaweed and surrounded by garbage.

As you journal, think about a time you felt vulnerable. Have you ever felt like you were wrapped in seaweed and surrounded by garbage? On a Post-it note, write the following sentence and place it on your mirror: "I am lifted up and carried by God" (Isaiah 63:9).

Let's Pray

Father, I am thankful I am the child of the King. I am blessed, I am redeemed, and I am forgiven. Please help me embrace and live in my new identity. In Jesus's name. Amen.

Write It Out!

Reflect on what God is speaking to your heart today.

Date:__________________________

Today I am feeling...

What one thing are you thankful for today?

Day Six

Dig Deeper

Read Genesis 4:1–16.

This is the result of competition and jealousy, which leads to division and destruction. Cain killed his brother because he felt jealousy over Abel's ability to please God. Cain didn't necessarily desire to please God, but he was jealous that Abel pleased Him. Cain wanted the praise without having to actually give God his heart and obedience. Cain was happy in his sin but not his status. Part of Cain's problem was his lack of faith and love. God knew the brothers' hearts, and Abel's faith made him righteous (Heb. 11:4). God doesn't just want our service—He wants our hearts and our love. Cain was convinced that killing his brother would end his problems, but it just made them worse.

We need to remember that God has given us special talents and assignments. No one can steal the destiny God has laid out for us. Some are meant to work quietly behind the scenes, and some in front of the crowds, but it doesn't mean anyone is less valuable. As God works and refines a willing person, their roles may change. A sculptor doesn't place an unchiseled rock in the gallery. It is only placed in the gallery after it is refined.

Are you serving and worshiping in a balanced fashion? Martha is a good reminder of the need for a healthy balance between giving God not only our hands in service but our hearts in worship.[15]

As you journal today, write about the balance of service and worship in your walk with God. On a Post-it note, write the following sentence and place it on your mirror: "I am refined by God" (Isaiah 48:10).

Let's Pray

Father, I desire to walk in perfect harmony with You. Please help me balance the service I offer with the worship I give. Help me love my fellow Christian and not envy them for the gifts they possess. I pray this in Jesus's name. Amen.

Write It Out

Reflect on what God is speaking to your heart today.

Date:__________________________

Today I am feeling...

What one thing are you thankful for today?

Day Seven

Today is a day to rest and reflect. This is a great day to complete the End of Week Goal Tracker and see your progress. Use the section below for sermon notes, rest in the Lord, and enjoy your family.

Write It Out!

Reflect on what God is speaking to your heart today.

Date:________________________

Sermon Notes:

Prayer Journal

What are you praying for? Write your prayers here. As your prayers are answered, jot down the day and how God answered. Was it what you prayed for or something better?

I am praying that God will…	Date	God answered by…

Who will you pray for this week?

Person/Organization:

Need:

Person/Organization:

Need:

"Nothing binds me to my Lord like a strong belief in His changeless love."

—Charles Spurgeon

Week Eleven

Day One

Isaiah 49:15 NLT
Can a mother forget her nursing child?
Can she feel no love for the child she has borne?

Study

A special bond forms when a mother carries a child for nine months. But I can also attest that a mother doesn't have to carry a child to love the child deeply. When a child is adopted with the right heart, they are loved as deeply as any natural-born child.

There are so many stories of adoption in the Bible. One of the greats is how God caused Pharoah's daughter to love and adopt Moses. For her to pluck him from the water and adopt him at a time when her father was killing baby boys could only be God's hand. God knows our hearts and character, and His plan will always be done.

The Lord knew that Joseph was the perfect man to adopt and raise His Son, and He knows the perfect task for you. It doesn't mean it will be easy, but it will be perfect.

A friend and I recently discussed serving with the right heart. My friend knows someone with a deep disdain for God but loves giving to the homeless. As a new Christian, he struggles with understanding why God will not pardon this person on judgment day. In his eyes, this person is a kind and loving soul because she shows compassion for the homeless. He sees her provide for their desperate needs, but he doesn't see the condition of her heart. God alone sees the motivation behind the action.

As you journal today, reflect on the purpose God has for you. On a Post-it note, write the following sentence and place it on your mirror: "I am justified" (Rom. 5:1).

Let's Pray

Lord, I know Your plan is perfect, and Your love is without measure. I pray for the lost today. I pray for the opportunity and the words to share the message that will lead them to You. In Jesus's name. Amen.

Write It Out!

Reflect on what God is speaking to your heart today.

Date:____________________________

Today I am feeling...

What one thing are you thankful for today?

Day Two

Ephesians 5:25 NKJV
Husbands, love your wives, just as Christ also loved the church and gave Himself for her.

Study

We live in a world that wants to twist and distort God's design. Satan tries to blind humanity with phrases like "Love is love." However, in the end, that won't fly with God. We are living in the days of deception, and the Bible said there would be days like this (1 Tim. 4:1).

But don't despair. Just because the sinful are unprotected doesn't mean you are unprotected. We are the bride of Christ. If an earthly groom loves and protects his bride, imagine how much Christ loves and protects us. Christ is the perfect Groom.

We are all at different points in life. Some seek earthly love, but as Christians, we live in love. If this is true, why do some still feel unloved? Like I said earlier, love is an action—it takes effort.

If you don't feed earthly love, it stops growing. Likewise, if you don't feed your spirit with God's love, it doesn't grow. We can't walk through life expecting others to fill us with love, and we can't give and receive lasting love without filling our spirit with God's love. We must feed our spirit. How do we feed our spirit? God's Word and prayer.

As you journal today, evaluate your relationship with the Lord. Are you reading His Word and seeking His counsel daily? On a Post-it note, write the following sentence and place it on your mirror: "I am filled with God's Spirit" (Romans 5:5).

Let's Pray

Father, I desire to have a close relationship with You. I know I will never be able to give or receive real love without You. As I draw closer, please fill me with Your perfect peace and love. Help me see others the way You see them. And help me embrace the fact that I am Your adopted child and filled with Your Spirit. I pray this in Jesus's name. Amen.

Write It Out!

Reflect on what God is speaking to your heart today.

Date:__________________________

Today I am feeling...

What one thing are you thankful for today?

Day Three

John 15:13 ESV
Greater love has no one than this,
that someone lay down his life for his friends.

Study

Have you ever had a friend you would give up everything for? Ruth and Naomi did. They had a close relationship because they were together daily. Judging by Ruth's decision to follow Naomi, they were closer to each other than blood relatives.

I had a close friend in high school, and we did everything together. The funny thing is a lot of people knew our names but didn't know which name went with which person. As it happens, we grew apart when I married and moved away. For years, I considered her my best friend, but she moved on. When we saw each other again, she introduced me as "someone she knew in high school," and I was hurt. But why was I surprised? When we grow apart from someone, we don't know who that person is anymore.

Laying down your life for another doesn't just mean taking a bullet and dying. Laying down your life can also mean wanting the best for someone else—wanting the best enough to forgo your personal interests. It's human nature to clutch onto what we have and hold dear. So, when we put others' interests above ours, we are taking a proverbial bullet for them. We are showing them God's love.

You are free because you have a Friend Who selflessly died for you.

As you journal today, reflect on the precious blood of Christ. How would your life be different if you didn't know Jesus? On a Post-it note, write the following sentence and place it on your mirror: "I am a friend of God because I know Him and follow His voice" (John 15:14).

Let's Pray

Jesus, thank You for salvation. Thank you for dying on the cross to wash me clean. Please forgive me for times when I forget to be thankful for Your sacrifice. In Jesus's name. Amen.

Write It Out!

Reflect on what God is speaking to your heart today.

Date:__________________________

Today I am feeling...

What one thing are you thankful for today?

Day Four

Mark 12:31 NKJV
And the second, like it, is this:
"You shall love your neighbor as yourself."
There is no other commandment greater than these.

Study

It's difficult to love someone you don't know. But it is the second most important thing to God. Esther faced death to follow God's directive.

Esther was Mordecai's orphaned niece, who, by God's plan, replaced Queen Vashti after she insulted the king. Like a fairytale story, Esther was the poor girl who won the heart of the king and became a queen. But it was God's plan, and it was no fairytale. King Xerxes made a man named Haman his most powerful official, and everyone was supposed to bow to him. When Esther's uncle refused to bow to him, Haman plotted to kill Mordecai and all the Jewish people. Haman convinced the king, and a decree to follow Haman's plan was delivered to each province (Est 3). Esther was the only person in a position to stop the slaughter of her people, but she would have to face possible death to follow God's directive.

You don't have to be a queen to be used by God. Even the tiniest of stones makes a ripple in the water. When someone loses a loved one or is facing their own death and still gives glory to God, they have impact. Our words and actions in times of trial lead others to Christ.

As you journal today, think of a situation that needs a fresh perspective. Is your trial worth the pain if it brings one person to Christ? On a Post-it note, write the following sentence and place it on your mirror: "I am protected by God" (Romans 8:28).

Let's Pray

Father, I know I will never see my life as You do. I don't have the ability to see the entire picture and may never understand the purpose of my trial. However, I choose to trust Your plan and follow wherever You lead. In Jesus's name, I pray. Amen.

Write It Out!

Reflect on what God is speaking to your heart today.

Date:________________________

Today I am feeling...

What one thing are you thankful for today?

Day Five

John 16:27 NLT
For the Father himself loves you dearly because you love me and believe that I came from God.

Study

As Christians, how do we show our love for Jesus? The lost world is always on the lookout for the fallen Christian. They are always ready to pounce and make a public spectacle of a follower's bad behavior.

As we tick closer to the end, this will only increase. Jesus spoke about a great apostasy, or "falling away" from the faith (Matt. 24:10–12). Yep, the Bible said there would be days like this. As things progress, Matthew 24:12 says the love of many will turn cold.

In the *Pilgrim's Progress* movie, Christian is constantly sidetracked by evil. At one point in the story, he meets up with a man named Faithful, and they enter the city called Vanity Fair. The two are told they can purchase anything desired there. It doesn't go over well when the men inform the inhabitants they are mistaken. They couldn't purchase what God had to offer there.

When the townspeople hear this, they are angered and take them to court. The judge sentences them to death, and while Christian waits in a cell, Faithful is burned at the stake.

God never promises our lives will be easy (John 16:33). It was the end of Faithful's journey, but God provided a way for Christian to escape, and in the process, a guard from Vanity Fair was saved. There is always a plan, and God is always in control.

As you journal today, praise God for the wonderful promise of heaven. On a Post-it note, write the following sentence and place it on your mirror: "I am filled with hope" (Psalm 62:5).

Let's Pray

Father, You are always in control. You guide my steps daily and bring me into contact with the lost and hopeless people in this world. Help me shine Your light in this dark world. In Jesus's name, I pray. Amen.

Write It Out!

Reflect on what God is speaking to your heart today.

Date:__________________________

Today I am feeling...

What one thing are you thankful for today?

Day Six

Dig Deeper

Read 1 Corinthians 13:4–7 and 1 John 4:8.

Our sins bring trial and punishment. The sins of Judah sent them into captivity by the Babylonians. However, God never abandoned His people. He is always faithful in love, even when life's journey turns treacherous. We have hope because of God's love.

In the *Pilgrim's Progress* movie, Christian gained insight into what he would face on his way to heaven. He saw a vision of an old man sitting alone in a cage and repeating the words, "No hope!" The man wouldn't move. He sat there desperately repeating the phrase with his head in his hands. Despite the cage's open door, he remained stuck because he had no hope. He was locked in a prison of his making because of his stinking thinking.

The enemy does everything in his power to make people turn from God. He uses people's selfish desires and vanity to lead them down the wrong path. Then he uses their desperation to make them give up.

What hope do we have in a fragile salvation? Salvation is a gift from God and, once accepted, is irrevocable (Romans 11:29). It is the devil's desire to make us feel hopeless and unloved. But with God's Spirit, we are firm in our salvation. And when we have the right outlook, we face trials differently. Our strength comes from the Lord, and when we rely on Him in hopeful anticipation, we face trouble with confidence.

As you journal today, thank God for His irrevocable gift of salvation. On a Post-it note, write the following sentence and place it on your mirror: "I am a daughter of the King" (Gal. 4:7).

Let's Pray

Jesus, thank You for dying on the cross for me. Your sacrifice demonstrates Your great love. Please help me show love to others. Help me walk confidently in my true identity. In Jesus's name. Amen.

Write It Out!

Reflect on what God is speaking to your heart today.

Date:__________________________

Today I am feeling...

What one thing are you thankful for today?

Day Seven

Today is a day to rest and reflect. This is a great day to complete the End of Week Goal Tracker and see your progress. Use the section below for sermon notes, rest in the Lord, and enjoy your family.

Write It Out!

Reflect on what God is speaking to your heart today.

Date:______________________

Sermon Notes:

Prayer Journal

What are you praying for? Write your prayers here. As your prayers are answered, jot down the day and how God answered. Was it what you prayed for or something better?

I am praying that God will…	Date	God answered by…

Who will you pray for this week?

Person/Organization:

Need:

Person/Organization:

Need:

"The great of this world are those who simply loved God more than others did."

—A.W. Tozer

Week Twelve

Day One

Jude 1:21 ESV
Keep yourselves in the love of God,
waiting for the mercy of our Lord
Jesus Christ that leads to eternal life.

Study

My transition from middle to high school was rough. I entered my freshmen year without friends. I don't remember why, but for some reason, my middle school friends ditched me. However, shortly after school started, I made friends with an upperclassman who was friends with the "bad kids."

The group smoked pot and hung out in the empty lot across the street from the school. And while I never took drugs, I did follow their directive on stealing. We regularly walked into the local grocery store and swiped snacks. My mom had no idea.

Some people find sin fun and exciting; the more we engage in it, the less it bothers us. We become desensitized to it. If left unchecked, those small sins must be replaced by bigger, more dangerous ones.

Thankfully, by my sophomore year, those kids were no longer my "friends." Since God controls everything, I must give Him the glory for changing my course. I found new friends and started in a new direction. It's like a snake shedding its skin and being renewed.

When you keep yourself in God's love, you are assured His mercy. He will direct your path and open doors for you to enter.

As you journal today, reflect on how God has, or is, changing your course. What doors are being opened? On a Post-it note, write the following sentence and place it on your mirror: "I am renewed in my spirit daily" (2 Cor. 4:16).

Let's Pray

Father, thank You for leading me down the right paths and keeping me safe as I journey closer to glory. Help me feel love in Your presence today and give love to others. I pray this in Jesus's name. Amen.

Write It Out!

Reflect on what God is speaking to your heart today.

Date:__________________________

Today I am feeling...

What one thing are you thankful for today?

Day Two

John 13:34 NLT
So now I am giving you a new commandment: Love each other. Just as I have loved you, you should love each other.

Study

There are so many in this world who believe the lie that God does not love them. The enemy is the "father of lies" (John 8:44). He uses lies to make us doubt God's love. I can imagine the lies flying around Martha when she found out her brother Lazarus was dead. But her faith wasn't shaken. Martha knew Who Jesus was, and she trusted in His wisdom and power to handle the situation. Jesus knows what is best for you. He knows your situation and knows you by name.

Have you ever had someone not know your name? After our mom died, our dad started to rapidly decline. It wasn't long before we were hearing the word Alzheimer's. I remember showing up at the home he was in, and he asked, "Are you the therapist?" I took him for a drive that day, and about every twenty minutes, he would look over and ask, "And who are you again?" It is heartbreaking when a parent doesn't know their child. On judgment day, some will stand before God, and He won't know them. But we can rejoice! If we are saved, we can look forward to the Father knowing us by name.

Imagine how wonderful that day will be. You are a child of the King, and you will receive your inheritance (1 Peter 1:4). You are running a race for God's glory, and there will be a reward for you in heaven.

As you journal today, reflect on how you are following God's plan for your life. On a Post-it note, write the following sentence and place it on your mirror: "I am victorious in Christ" (1 Cor. 15:57).

Let's Pray

Father, I desire to fulfill the plan You have for my life. Please help me as I walk the way You have for me. Guide me down the right paths and help me focus on You as I reflect Your love to the world. In Jesus's name, I pray. Amen.

Write It Out!

Reflect on what God is speaking to your heart today.

Date:__________________________

Today I am feeling...

What one thing are you thankful for today?

Day Three

Deuteronomy 10:12 NIV
And now, Israel, what does the Lord your God ask of you but to fear the Lord your God, to walk in obedience to him, to love him, to serve the Lord your God with all your heart and with all your soul.

Study

I heard a pastor speak who said our purpose on this earth is to spread God's love and His message of salvation. I think that sums it up well. In a world filled with anger and hate, the message of love is like a cool drink for the soul. But how do we trust God's leading, set aside fear, and boldly go where He asks us to go?

God does not give us a spirit of fear. But the enemy wants to keep us bound by fear. We suffer from fear of the unknown. What will others think or say? What if I make someone angry? We don't have to look far to see how satan controls the lost people in this world. As we draw closer to the end, we are inundated with hate.

Close your eyes and picture a dark stage. The stage of this world is cloaked in darkness. I see demons whispering in people's ears and, like zombies, people turn and follow evil directives. But do you see the light threatening the dome of darkness? It starts as a hairline crack, and like the fracture in a window, the fingers slowly break and spread in every direction. The dark cannot stop the fracture of light—with each crack, a radiant beam penetrates and illuminates. Darkness is just the absence of light. You are full of light.

As you journal today, release yourself from the things you cannot control. When you commit to reacting in love, you fulfill a purpose. On a Post-it note, write the following sentence and place it on your mirror: "I am made for a purpose" (Jer. 29:11).

Let's Pray

Father, thank You for the love You pour out and the hearts You change. I am not responsible for the state of others' hearts. Help me remember to react with love to every situation. In Jesus's name, I pray. Amen.

Write It Out!

Reflect on what God is speaking to your heart today.

Date:________________________

Today I am feeling...

What one thing are you thankful for today?

Day Four

Psalm 136:26 NIV
Give thanks to the God of heaven.
His love endures forever.

Study

God doesn't want us to live life in agony and then drag ourselves over the finish line, bruised and battered. There is no doubt we live in a broken world, but we don't have to allow it to break us. God sees you, and He loves you. Your circumstances do not define your worth. The lies the enemy has told you are to keep you from God's purpose.

The movie *Extraordinary* is based on the true story of a man who ran a 2,900-mile cross-country race. This would be a feat for anyone, but David Horton ran this race after having open-heart surgery and needing knee surgery. His wife was clueless about the knee surgery and was upset when he chose the race over a family vacation. As the movie progressed, their perspectives changed. David realized how much he loved his family, and his wife saw the greater purpose. As he ran, David led others to Christ.

You have a greater purpose than what you fully understand. God created you to do great things for His kingdom and glory. When you stand before God, He will say, "Well done, my good and faithful servant" (Matt 25:21 NLT).

As you journal today, think about your worship. Are you at the feet of Jesus daily? On a Post-it note, write the following sentence and place it on your mirror: "I am set apart and sanctified in truth" (John 17:18-19).

Let's Pray

Jesus, I desire to rest at Your feet. Help me put aside the concerns of this world and give You reverence. Please help me seek You in every season of my life and rest in Your love. I know You will keep me in perfect peace. In Jesus's name, I pray. Amen.

Write It Out

Reflect on what God is speaking to your heart today.

Date:________________________

Today I am feeling...

What one thing are you thankful for today?

Day Five

1 John 4:10 NLT
This is real love—not that we loved God, but that he loved us and sent his Son as a sacrifice to take away our sins.

Study

As we learn to allow healing in our lives, we become whole. The cracks in our souls are mended, and the love poured into us by God fills us. But change takes effort. For years, I went through the motions. I pulled my Bible off the shelf on Sunday and put it back for the rest of the week. I prayed when trouble came but forgot when times were good. I lived apart from God. That life left me on spiritual life support. My house was built on sand, and the slightest quake shook my faith. This isn't the life God wants for us.

Throughout the movie *Greater*, as Brandon's brother Marty sat with the devil who told him lies, football players placed flowers on the field for Brandon's funeral service. At the movie's end, Marty finally stood up, looked at the devil, and said, "I've had enough of your company today." At the top of the grandstands, Marty looked down at the field and saw the words formed from the flowers: "We Trust." Brandon was lost to the world, but he wasn't lost to the saved. A whole community trusted the promises of God. After reading those words, Marty ran to the gym where others celebrated the life of a great man. With love in his heart and joy shining on his face, Marty joined the celebration.

As you journal today, write out your hopeful expectations. Let hope heal your wounds and allow God to fill you. On a Post-it note, write the following sentence and place it on your mirror: "I am filled with peace" (Lam. 3:24, Rom. 15:13).

Let's Pray

Father, You are the only One who can heal me and satisfy me. Please heal my wounds and fill me with peace, love, hope, and joy. I pray this, in Jesus's name. Amen.

Write It Out!

Reflect on what God is speaking to your heart today.

Date:__________________________

Today I am feeling...

What one thing are you thankful for today?

Day Six

Dig Deeper

Read Romans 8:26–39 and Galatians 5:22–26.

The Holy Spirit enables us to love others appropriately regardless of the love they return—not to be a doormat, but to be a light.

As Christians, we go through stages of development. The stages of a butterfly's life come to my mind. The process of going from an egg to a caterpillar to a beautiful butterfly can easily represent the stages we experience as Christians. Once encapsulated, the caterpillar releases digestive juices that begin to break down its body. The caterpillar's form changes into a soupy substance, and out of that soup, emerges as a beautiful butterfly.

Just as the caterpillar changes into a butterfly, through salvation, we are changed by Christ. However, unlike the butterfly, we determine the extent of our metamorphosis. We are saved, but the growth we experience is up to us.

As you walk through life, understanding what love is and where it comes from, you are set free. Your worthiness for love is no longer determined by a person's sinful, selfish standards. Therefore, you have the assurance that you are fully and perfectly loved.

Today, gather the *I am* statements you have written over the past few weeks, and write each statement on a single piece of paper. As you write each one, reflect on the meaning of the words you write. Add this statement to the bottom: "I am filled with love and joy" (Gal 5:22). Paste the page to your mirror and repeat these *I am* statements daily.

As you journal today, write about your identity in Christ.

Let's Pray

Father, thank You for my identity in You. I have been washed clean, and I am living with Your Spirit in me. Thank You for filling me with Your love. In Jesus's name I pray. Amen.

Write It Out!

Reflect on what God is speaking to your heart today.

Date:________________________

Today I am feeling...

What one thing are you thankful for today?

Day Seven

Today is a day to rest and reflect. This is a great day to complete the End of Week Goal Tracker and see your progress. Use the section below for sermon notes, rest in the Lord, and enjoy your family.

Write It Out!

Reflect on what God is speaking to your heart today.

Date:______________________

Sermon Notes:

Prayer Journal

What are you praying for? Write your prayers here. As your prayers are answered, jot down the day and how God answered. Was it what you prayed for or something better?

I am praying that God will…	Date	God answered by…

Who will you pray for this week?

Person/Organization:

Need:

Person/Organization:

Need:

Thank You

Again, I give God the glory for this book. I have wanted to quit many times but continue on with God's grace. The Lord keeps me in peace as I humbly work to write what He lays on my heart.

Thanks to Andrea Lende for helping me refine the words on these pages. She is my cheerleader, and I value her friendship and support.

I also want to thank Lyneta Smith for her willingness to edit this book and *Seeking Peace in Every Season*. I am blessed to know her.

I want to thank everyone who has supported and encouraged me. There are too many to mention here, but each one is valued. I thank God for each of you.

Bibliography

Answers in Genesis. *"1061. Rahab."* Charles H. Spurgeon. Accessed January 11, 2024. https://answersingenesis.org/education/spurgeon-sermons/1061-rahab/.

———. "The Walls of Jericho." Bryant Wood. Accessed January 11, 2024. https://answersingenesis.org/archaeology/the-walls-of-jericho/.

Arkansasrazorbacks.com. "'Greater'—A True Story Worthy Of Hollywood." Kevin Trainor. Accessed January 20, 2024. https://arkansasrazorbacks.com/greater-brandon-burlsworth-movie-2/.

BetterHelp. *"Why It's Important To Love People."* Accessed January 7, 2024. https://www.betterhelp.com/advice/love/why-its-important-to-love-people/#.

Bible Study Tools. "Who Was Mary Magdalene in the Bible?" Meg Bucher. Accessed January 6, 2024. https://www.biblestudytools.com/bible-study/topical-studies/who-was-mary-magdalene.html.

———. "Genesis 25:21 Meaning and Commentary." Accessed January 20, 2024. https://www.biblestudytools.com/msg/genesis/25-21.html.

Block, Daniel I. *Judges, Ruth: An Exegetical and Theological Exposition of Holy Scripture (Volume 6) The New American Commentary.* Nashville: Broadman & Holman Publishers, 1999.

Bodenhamer, Kim Williams. "Book of Ruth" in *The Lexham Bible Dictionary,* ed. John D. Barry et al. Bellingham, WA: Lexham Press, 2016.

Chapman, Gary. *The 5 Love Languages: The Secret to Love That Lasts.* Chicago: Northfield Publishing, 1992.

———. *The Heart of The 5 Love Languages.* Chicago, IL: Northfield Publishing, 2007.

Dove.org. "*Great*er." Accessed January 20, 2024. https://dove.org/review/11995-greater/.

Facebook. *"Lee Strobel—The Unexpected Adventure: Easter."* Accessed February 1, 2024. https://www.facebook.com/valleychurchdm/videos/1015610429818473l/.

Fazekas, Steve. n.d. *Slaughter at Jericho.* Accessed January 11, 2024. https://answersingenesis.org/contradictions-in-the-bible/slaughter-at-jericho/.

Florida Museum. "Butterfly Life Cycle." Accessed February 19, 2024. https://www.floridamuseum.ufl.edu/educators/resource/butterfly-life-cycle/#:~:text=Butterflies%20and%20moths%20undergo%20a,the%20life%20of%20the%20insect.

Focus on the Family. "Submission of Wives to Husbands." Accessed January 12, 2024. https://www.focusonthefamily.com/family-qa/submission-of-wives-to-husbands/.

Ginger. "Wake up on the Wrong Side of the Bed." Accessed January 17, 2024. https://www.gingersoftware.com/content/phrases/wake-up-on-the-wrong-side-of-the-bed#.

Got Questions. "Summary of the Book of Deuteronomy." Accessed January 19, 2024. https://www.gotquestions.org/Book-of-Deuteronomy.html.

———. "What Can We Learn from the Woman at the Well?" Accessed January 3, 2024. https://www.gotquestions.org/woman-at-the-well.html.

———. "What Can We Learn from the Woman Caught in Adultery?" Accessed January 3, 2024. https://www.gotquestions.org/woman-caught-in-adultery.html.
———. "What Does It Mean That Faith, Hope, and Love Remain (1 Corinthians 13:13)?" Accessed January 4, 2024. https://www.gotquestions.org/faith-hope-love.html.
———. "What Does the Bible Say about How Widows Are to Be Treated?" Accessed January 7, 2024. https://www.gotquestions.org/Bible-widows.html.
———. "What Does the Bible Say about the Virgin Mary?" Accessed January 29, 2024. https://www.gotquestions.org/virgin-Mary.html.
———. "What Is the Meaning of the Story of the Woman with the Issue of Blood?" Accessed January 4, 2024. https://www.gotquestions.org/woman-issue-blood.html.
———. "What Is the Story of Jacob, Leah, and Rachel?" Accessed January 23, 2024. https://www.gotquestions.org/Jacob-Leah-Rachel.html.
———. "What Was the Story of Jacob and Esau?" Accessed January 22, 2024. https://www.gotquestions.org/Jacob-and-Esau.html.
———. "*Who Am I in Christ?"* Accessed January 30, 2024. https://www.gotquestions.org/who-in-Christ.html.
———. "Who Was Abigail in the Bible?" Accessed January 9, 2024. https://www.gotquestions.org/Abigail-in-the-Bible.html.
———. "Who Was Gomer in the Bible?" Accessed January 9, 2024. https://www.gotquestions.org/Gomer-in-the-Bible.html.
———. "Who Was Martha in the Bible?" Accessed February 29, 2024. https://www.gotquestions.org/Martha-in-the-Bible.html.
———. "Who Was Mary of Bethany in the Bible?" Accessed February 5, 2024. https://www.gotquestions.org/life-Mary-Bethany.html.
———. "Who Was Rahab in the Bible?" Accessed December 2023. https://www.gotquestions.org/life-Rahab.html.
———. "Who Was Ruth in the Bible?" Accessed January 2024. https://www.gotquestions.org/life-Ruth.html.

———. "Who Was Sarah in the Bible?" Accessed January 18, 2024. https://www.gotquestions.org/life-Sarah.html.

———. "Who was Tamar in the Bible?" Accessed January 7, 2024. https://www.gotquestions.org/Tamar-Bible.html.

———. "Why Did God Love Jacob and Hate Esau?" Accessed January 22, 2024. https://www.gotquestions.org/Jacob-Esau-love-hate.html.

Patterns of Evidence. "3,500-Year-Old News of the Red Sea Miracle." Dr. R. Brian Rickett. Accessed January 11, 2024. https://www.patternsofevidence.com/2020/05/15/3500-year-old-news-red-sea-miracle/.

Popkin, Shannon. *Control Girl: Lessons on Surrendering Your Burden of Control from Seven Women in the Bible.* Grand Rapids: Kregel Publications, 2017.

Psychology Today. "*Choosing Gratitude and Optimism.*" Gregory L. Jantz, Ph. D. Accessed January 18, 2024. https://www.psychologytoday.com/us/blog/hope-relationships/202008/choosing-gratitude-and-optimism.

Sermons by Logos. "Mary Magdalene." Daniel Bryan. Accessed January 6, 2024. https://sermons.logos.com/sermons/912449-mary-magdalene.

Endnotes

[1]"What Can We Learn from the Woman at the Well?," Got Questions, accessed January 3, 2024, https://www.gotquestions.org/woman-at-the-well.html.

[2] "Why It's Important To Love People," BetterHelp, accessed January 7, 2024, https://www.betterhelp.com/advice/love/why-its-important-to-love-people/#.

[3] "Who Was Abigail in the Bible?," Got Questions, accessed January 9, 2024, https://www.gotquestions.org/Abigail-in-the-Bible.html.

[4] "Who Was Gomer in the Bible?," Got Questions, accessed January 9, 2024, https://www.gotquestions.org/Gomer-in-the-Bible.html.

[5] "Slaughter at Jericho," Steve Fazekas, Answers in Genesis, accessed January 11, 2024, https://answersingenesis.org/contradictions-in-the-bible/slaughter-at-jericho/.

[6] "3,500-Year-Old News of the Red Sea Miracle," Dr. R. Brian Rickett, Patterns of Evidence, accessed January 11, 2024, https://www.patternsofevidence.com/2020/05/15/3500-year-old-news-red-sea-miracle/.

[7] "1061. Rahab," Charles H. Spurgeon, Answers in Genesis, accessed January 11, 2024, https://answersingenesis.org/education/spurgeon-sermons/1061-rahab/.

[8] Gary Chapman, The Heart of The 5 Love Languages (Chica go, IL: Northfield Publishing, 2007), 8.

[9]Shannon Popkin, Control Girl (Grand Rapids: Kregel Publica tions, 2017), 58.

[10] "Choosing Gratitude and Optimism," Gregory L. Jantz, Ph. D., Psychology Today, accessed January 18, 2024, https://www.psychologytoday.com/us/blog/hope-relationships/202008/choosing-gratitude-and-optimism.

[11] "Who Was Sarah in the Bible?," Got Questions, accessed January 18, 2024, https://www.gotquestions.org/life-Sarah.html.

[12] "Greater," Dove.org, accessed January 20, 2024, https://dove.org/review/11995-greater/.

[13] "Who Am I in Christ?," Got Questions, accessed January 30, 2024, https://www.gotquestions.org/who-in-Christ.html.

[14] "Lee Strobel—The Unexpected Adventure: Easter," Face book, accessed February 1, 2024, https://www.face book.com/valleychurchdm/videos/10156104298184731/.

[15] "Who Was Martha in the Bible?," Got Questions, accessed February 29, 2024, https://www.gotquestions.org/Mar tha-in-the-Bible.html.

About The Author

Tracey Glenn is a born-again child of God and a Jesus freak. She is a writer, speaker, and seeker of biblical wisdom. With a heart for God, kids, and all God's creatures, Tracey shares her journey through the pages of her life as one who loves the Lord. She is a graduate of the School of Hard Knocks, and the Lord has used that education to transform her into a new creation. Tracey has an associate degree in psychology and graphic design, has completed the Living Waters School of Biblical Evangelism, and is a successful entrepreneur.

Raised on a cattle ranch in southeast Arizona, Tracey has been married for thirty-five years to the love of her life, Link, and she is a mother of three and grandmother of four. She has raised a child with special needs and is currently homeschooling her adopted son. She cofounded a business in 2007, which currently has five locations across southern Arizona and provides other special needs children and their families with essential support and services. Helping others in need ultimately led her and her husband to adopt their son in 2013. You can learn more about Tracey and book her to speak on her website www.traceyglenn.com, or connect with her on Facebook @traceyglenn author speaker or Instagram @brandedinfaith.

Tracey Glenn books:

Gathering the Wayward Heart: Lessons on Faith, Trust, and Surrendering Our Best-Laid Plans;

We Get You!: 30 Days, 30 Women, 30 Stories, One God;

Seeking Peace in Every Season: 12-Week Devotional, Journal, and Planner

Visit www.traceyglenn.com for her latest Free offer!